VOICES FROM GENESIS

GUIDING US THROUGH THE STAGES OF LIFE

In an innovative tour-de-force, Norman Cohen—one of the par-ticipants in Bill Moyers' *Genesis: A Living Conversation* series on PBS—brings the leading figures of Genesis to new life.

In *Voices from Genesis*, the characters in these enthralling biblical stories—from Adam and Eve through Abraham and Sarah, Isaac and Rebekkah, Jacob, Rachel and Leah, and Joseph—speak directly to us about their spiritual and emotional journeys, struggles, frustrations, and confusions. We see how their experiences resurface in each of our lives.

Providing the framework for Cohen's approach are the insights of Erik Erikson, a twentieth-century legend in the field of developmental psychology, who viewed culture and society as key factors in shaping personality. Cohen applies each of Erikson's eight stages of human development to Genesis' characters so that each comes to represent a different stage in life—from birth to maturity to death.

In no other book of the Bible do characters move so fully through their different life stages. *Voices from Genesis* can teach us how to:

• Better understand ourselves and others.
• Improve our relationships.
• Cope with the stresses and struggles of our everyday lives.
• Carry the wisdom of Genesis through the present day.

"What Cohen gives us here is a powerful sense of the humanity of these earliest biblical figures, faults and all."

—*The Jerusalem Report*

DR. NORMAN J. COHEN is Acting President of Hebrew Union College–Jewish Institute of Religion and Professor of Midrash. He lectures widely on the topic of *midrash*—finding contemporary meaning from ancient biblical texts. Cohen was a participant in Bill Moyers' *Genesis: A Living Conversation* series on PBS. His previous books include *Masking and Unmasking Ourselves: Interpreting Biblical Texts on Clothing & Identity; Self, Struggle & Change: Family Conflict Stories in Genesis and Their Healing Insights for Our Lives* and *The Way Into Torah* (all Jewish Lights Publishing).

"A clearly delineated and persuasive guide to studying the Torah.... Highly recommended."

—*Library Journal*

For People of All Faiths, All Backgrounds

JEWISH LIGHTS Publishing

www.jewishlights.com

 Find us on Facebook®
Facebook is a registered
trademark of Facebook, Inc.

COVER DESIGN: DRENA FAGEN

COVER ART: *MISHKAN NO. I* BY ROBERT DOV TENNENBAUM

(Side view of the Tabernacle *Mishkan* inside the court enclosure)

Voices from Genesis

Guiding Us Through the Stages of Life

Norman J. Cohen

Jewish Lights Publishing

Voices from Genesis
Guiding Us Through the Stages of Life

Copyright © 1998 by Norman J. Cohen

Library of Congress Cataloging-in-Publication Data

Cohen, Norman J.
Voices from Genesis : guiding us through the stages of life /
by Norman J. Cohen.
p.   cm.
Includes bibliographical references.
ISBN 1-879045-75-3 (hardcover)
1. Bible. O.T. Genesis—Psychology. 2. Bible. O.T. Genesis—Biography.
3. Life cycle, Human—Religious aspects—Judaism. 4. Developmental psychology.
I. Title.
BS1235.6.P9C65   1998
222'.1106—DC21   98–35476   CIP

First Edition

ISBN 978-1-68336-473-3 (hc)
ISBN 978-1-58023-118-3 (pbk)

Manufactured in the United States of America

Design template by Glenn Suokko
Typesetting by Doug Porter
Jacket designed by Drena Fagen
Cover art by Robert Dov Tennenbaum, artist.
Side view of the tabernacle (*Mishkan*)
inside the court enclosure.

For People of All Faiths, All Backgrounds
Published by Jewish Lights Publishing

www.jewishlights.com

To the memory of my parents,

Molly and Irving Cohen.

They lavished me with their affection, love,
caring, and concern, as well as their
deep commitment to Judaism
and the Jewish People.

Contents

Preface   9

Introduction   11

Foreword   17

CHAPTER ONE: ADAM AND EVE
Infancy   21

CHAPTER TWO: CAIN AND ABEL
Early Childhood   33

CHAPTER THREE: NOAH
Play Age   47

CHAPTER FOUR: THE PEOPLE OF SHINAR
                    (and the Tower of Babel)
Pre-Adolescence   59

CHAPTER FIVE: ABRAHAM
Adolescence   69

CHAPTER SIX: ISAAC
The Young Adult   93

CHAPTER SEVEN: THE YOUNG JACOB
Maturity   111

CHAPTER EIGHT: THE OLDER JACOB
Old Age   135

POSTSCRIPT: THE LIFE OF JOSEPH
The Journey of the Jewish People   151

Appendix   155

Endnotes   156

Suggested Further Reading   178

About Jewish Lights Publishing   180

Preface

This book speaks about the human journey from birth to death as reflected in the development of the characters in the Book of Genesis. As such, it challenges all conscientious readers to reflect upon their lives and the stages of growth which they have experienced. Our personal journeys, no matter how diverse, share many things in common. Our parents and siblings, for example, are the strongest factors that determine our personae and our modes of interacting with the world. Even as we develop over the years, we often continue to wrestle with what our family represents for us.

I was blessed in my life to have had two loving parents whose major goal in life was to do the best they could in every way for my brother Marvin and for me. Molly and Irving Cohen z"l, whose memory I cherish and whose presence I miss, were loving parents who were generous in the love, devotion, time, and energy they gave to each of us. They rarely thought primarily of themselves, believing that their first responsibility was to provide their children with a home and support which would enable them to grow and mature into productive and caring adults in their own right. They were concerned not only about our growth as human beings, intellectually and emotionally, but were also determined that we find meaningful Jewish paths for ourselves. Whether it was encouraging us to become involved in the Zionist movement and experiencing the miracle of the Land of Israel, or to attend Hebrew high school after becoming bar mitzvah so we would take Jewish learning seriously, they were devoted to ensuring that their sons would be knowledgeable, active, and proud Jews. And they delighted in the fact that I became a rabbi and continued studying Judaica/Hebraica seriously, and that Marvin made *aliyah*, served in the Israeli Air Force, and studied medicine at Ben Gurion University. It is a blessing that my father lived to see his two sons embark on their career paths and create families of their own. My mother died too young to see the full blossoming of what they had a hand in shaping.

My brother Marvin, who is now a highly successful anesthesiologist, is a powerful model for me of a passionate Jew who loves everything about Judaism. Though we are not geographically close, we have always been close spiritually. This provides me not only with a link to our past, but grounds me as we look to the future.

The journey that has culminated in the creation of *Voices from Genesis* was shaped in large measure by the three individuals with whom I grew up. However, several individuals associated with Jewish Lights Publishing played a major role in its seeing the light of day. I owe much to Arthur Magida, who served as the editor of the book. His insights, questioning, and strong editorial hand have made it immeasurably better. Stuart Matlins, the founder of Jewish Lights, friend, colleague, and mentor in many ways, has helped me find my own voice to express to a wide audience my passion for Torah and its meaning in my life.

In sharing this journey through Genesis with you, I offer you a prism through which to view your own life. May you see reflected in it who you are and who you hope to become. "By Your light do we see light." (Psalm 36:10)

N.J.C.
Yorktown Heights, N.Y.
8 Nissan, 5758
Yahrzeit of my father, Irving Cohen z"l

Introduction

As we approach the end of the twentieth century and embark on a new millennium, we are seriously engaged in a search for meaning in our lives. This search takes cultural and religious forms and the need for it comes from our desire to make sense out of our own lives and to understand our place in the continuum of life. Art, literature, myths, religion, philosophy, and psychotherapy are all forms we use to express our questions and yearnings, and give structure to our quest for self-understanding.[1]

This is especially true in the field of psychoanalysis, where many leading figures have focused their research and writing on the issues of human development. These include such well-known scholars as Jean Piaget, Robert Kegan, Robert Havighurst, and Jane Loevinger, to name a few, though Erik Erikson continues to be most closely identified with the attempt to outline the stages of human growth.[2]

Erikson augmented Freud's theories by emphasizing personality development as a dynamic interaction between the individual and his environment. For Erikson, culture and society are key factors that shape personality. Personality, he wrote, is not determined solely by the parent-child relationship, but continues to develop throughout the entire life cycle. Ongoing life experiences feed into the shaping of our ego-identity. Erikson set this psycho-social understanding of human development into an eight-stage theory, with our progression through the stages dependent upon how well we have negotiated each previous stage.

The stage theory of Erikson is grounded on a principle which asserts that an organism becomes more and more differentiated over time. This is largely the result of external influences. This movement is characterized by emerging challenges at each stage. These turning points in our development are experienced as tensions between positive and negative forces, which must be resolved if we are to grow. Wholeness, therefore, does not mean total freedom from conflict. The tensions or polarities in each of us must be continually resolved, and basic virtues emerge from these resolutions. Resolution is essential to enter the next potential stage of growth, though these crises are never totally settled, and each can be relived in future stages.

It is difficult to attach specific ages to each developmental stage, since each person progresses at his or her own pace. We might advance in spurts or even regress to an earlier stage when confronting difficult circumstances, and negative feelings and patterns of behavior can reappear when we feel threatened.[3]

Just as psychoanalysis is a vehicle for us to grapple with our development and understand it, so, too, are stories meant to provide us with ways to organize and deal with our life experiences which, to an extent, are inchoate.[4] Stories protect us from chaos, providing us with a foundation of memory and a potential for self-understanding. They are essential because they help us make sense of our lives.[5]

In particular, myths and sacred stories speak to the life journey that each of us makes. They embody events which take place in the psychic and spiritual life of all of us. Sacred stories also provide a sense of meaning to our own baffling dramas as they link us with past members of our community with whom we share a common destiny.[6] Perhaps few books can do this better than the Bible. By immersing ourselves in its sacred stories, whether we see them as divinely given or the inspired creations of human beings, we can find out about our own true natures; about who we are and who we can become.

According to the rabbinic understanding of the Bible, or Torah as it is traditionally known in Judaism, all human experience and knowledge is woven into its narrative fabric. The unfolding of history is evident in its sequence of events, just as all new, contemporary interpretations of the text are part of its original intent. All this was implicitly part of what was revealed at Sinai, though revelation is ongoing and mediated by the process of interpretation, which Judaism calls *midrash*.[7] Revelation is not something that occurs once—and never again. Every reader in every generation can draw new and poignant meaning from the biblical text.

The midrashic process is a dynamic interaction between the reader and the text, and the moment when the text and the reader meet is when meaning is born.[8] The reader doesn't merely read the biblical narrative, but rather *experiences* it. Its significance does not lie in the meaning sealed within the text, but rather in the fact that the text elicits what had been previously sealed within the reader.[9] What is hidden in the text is the reader's most essential and intimate life: his or her longings, fears, doubts, questions, and struggles.[10] It is these essential parts of ourselves which are uncovered when we become one with the text.

Reading the Bible, then, is about change. And this takes effort. Reading it involves one's entire being, and this forces involvement, response, passion, and self-reflection.[11]

As readers open their hearts, minds, and souls to the biblical text, the text reflects back to them their own struggles and dilemmas. And the more they reveal aspects of themselves while reading and interpreting the text, the more the text will affect them. Ultimately, as we create new meanings in our engagement with the Bible, this process transforms us. The text does not merely mirror back to us who we are, but also shows us who we can become.

Since we change over time as our relationships and circumstances change, the particular meaning that we create as we engage with the biblical text at any one moment may be different than any previous meaning. As we go through a series of transformations at different times in our lives, experiencing at each stage different conflicts, challenges, and life issues, we are inevitably drawn to different aspects of the biblical narrative and to different characters. We might also be drawn to different aspects in the life of a particular biblical personality.

The Bible reflects how characters change and grow over a lifetime. This is especially true of the Book of Genesis, where characters move through different life stages. Yet, if we look closely at them, we can discern that each character's story seems to focus upon the human struggle at one particular stage of that character's development. Moving from the birth of Adam and Eve to the death of Jacob, we see characters essentially growing and maturing through different stages in ways that resemble our own development throughout our own lives. Seen in this manner, the Genesis narrative, if read as a whole, portrays a series of characters who represent the life journey of one human being, from birth to death.[12] The fullness that was Adam was there in potential at the moment of his conception, and was revealed over time through the lives of his descendants. Adam embodied all human experience, and the Book of Genesis facilitates its unfolding.

When we confront the characters of Genesis and their life stories, we come in touch with our own journeys since the text mirrors who we are at any given stage of our development. We can see our changing selves in the different biblical stories and in the struggles of the characters. By immersing ourselves in the life moments of each biblical personality, this ancient text can help us understand and shape our own dramas. It can also help us to move to a greater sense of wholeness.

I propose, then, that our reading of Genesis be conditioned by two very different, yet powerful, sources of knowledge. First, that we focus upon Erik Erikson's understanding of the stages of human development and use it as a road map as we proceed through Genesis. To this end, I have divided the book into eight chapters which parallel Erikson's eight stages of human development. At the outset of each chapter is a brief summary of the particular stage. For the reader's further edification, I have appended a chart of Erikson's system at the conclusion of the book, to which the reader can refer.

However, our reading of Genesis cannot be shaped solely by our life experiences and the wisdom and insights of modern psychology. To have any authenticity and enduring value, our *midrash* must be moored in a clear understanding of the basic meaning of the biblical text and in the interpretive traditions of the past. This will set our interpretation in the continuum that stretches back to Mount Sinai. Therefore, I cite in the sidebars on each page all the sources which I have used, including the biblical passages and the midrashic texts. This will help the reader better understand how I have shaped my own reading of the characters in Genesis.

Yet, *my* reading of Genesis is simply my encounter with it through the prism of my knowledge and life experiences. That process of encounter is available to *every* inquisitive, thoughtful reader. Whenever a passionate reader engages with these sacred stories and finds that they apply to his or her life, the Torah is renewed. Each of us can experience revelation when we hear the voices of the text filtered through our own hearts and minds. At that moment, what was given implicitly to Moses at Sinai to transmit to the Jewish People, and to all humanity, is revealed—and the reader is transformed by it.

So then, let us listen attentively to the voices of Genesis, realizing that they speak of the times and struggles of our own lives. As they resonate with us, we can come to understand that the story which begins in the Garden of Eden with Adam and Eve and culminates with Jacob's death in Egypt is the journey of our lives. It is a journey which moves from birth, through infancy, childhood, and adolescence, to adulthood and old age, ending with our return to the Source of all being which grants us life and sustains us.

Foreword

"Jacob lived seventeen years in the land of Egypt, so that the span of his life came to one hundred and forty-seven years. And the time approached for Jacob to die."
—GENESIS 47:28–29

I found it difficult to breathe: I could feel my lungs struggling to fill with air as I tried to focus on the task at hand. Although I could not remember the last time I had been sick, the past few weeks had been difficult. It was impossible for me to get out of bed, and every movement caused me great pain. I now realized that I might not live to see the morning light.

The tent was pitch black as I waited for them to arrive. Yet, I was able to discern, perhaps for the first time in my 147 years, how my whole life fit together. It was not just that my entire life was arrayed before my very eyes, but I had a deep sense of how I was a link between my grandfather and my father, on the one hand, and my children, grandchildren, and all those who would come after them, on the other hand. I was overcome by the harmony I felt between my past and my tribe's future.

All of a sudden, the quiet was sharply broken by a voice. It was Joseph, Rachel's firstborn, who had brought his two sons, Ephraim and Manasseh, for my blessing. Summoning all the strength I could muster, I sat up in bed and looked at my Egyptian-born grandchildren. As I gazed at them, I couldn't help but think of my beloved Rachel, whom I had lost so many years before on the road to Ephrat as she gave birth to Joseph's brother Benjamin. And I thought about how hard it had been for me to raise my sons by myself.

brought his two sons...
Genesis 48:1–2.

whom I had lost...
Genesis 48:7.

My mind continued to wander back to my relationship with my brother Esau, whom I had not seen in years. I thought about how our father, Isaac, had blessed both of us. That is especially important to me now because I am about to bless Joseph's sons. I could see my mother Rebekkah's ashen face as she urged me to flee to Haran and go to her brother Laban's house after I had stolen the blessing meant for Esau. I even thought of my grandfather, Abraham, and the story that he had told us about how his family had moved from Aram Naharaim by the great rivers to the Land of Canaan and that God had promised to make us as numerous as the stars in the heavens and that our tribe would dwell on this land forever.

the great rivers...
The Tigris and Euphrates Rivers in Southern Mesopotamia.
numerous as the...
Genesis 15:5–7.

As I reached out to touch the heads of my two grandchildren, I could feel my grandfather, Abraham, gently rub my head as he regaled me with ancient stories of those who had come before him, of the early generations of humanity from which all tribes arose. I remembered hearing about the people of Shinar and how they erected a tower which reached to the heavens, and Noah's ark which survived the flood that God had brought to destroy the world. Staring at Ephraim and Manasseh, I couldn't help but think of the story of Cain and Abel, the first siblings, and how their struggle ended with the older brother killing the younger one. I even recalled how my grandfather had described a magnificent Garden that he called "Eden." God had placed the first human beings there after creating the world in six days. Eventually, God banished them from Eden to live in the world that we know, a world of pain, conflict, and joy.

In this one special moment, I could see the past, from the very beginning of time, as clearly as I could see the faces of my grandchildren who represented my future. And I understood more than ever that our family's destiny had been set in motion with the creation of Adam and Eve.

Knowing that I was about to die, I not only thought of my children's future, but I realized for the first time that I was the sum total of all the generations which preceded me. Not only was I linked directly to Isaac and Abraham, but all those who had come before—Noah, Seth, Cain, even Adam and Eve—were a part of me. Their voices were my voice, and when I blessed my children and my grandchildren, I would hear Adam Ha-Rishon, the first human being, speaking through the spirals of time.

CHAPTER ONE

ADAM AND EVE

Infancy

> ### *Erik Erikson: Stage One*
> ### *Basic Trust vs. Basic Mistrust*
>
> - The infant moves from a state of being merged with the mother to a state of being "in relation" to her. The mother's love affords the infant the security that enables him or her to move from dependence to autonomy.
> - There is a mutuality of recognition between the mother and the child—recognition by touch, face, name, and voice. They both develop as a result of their interaction.
> - The mother's task—to wean the child—leads to a sense of separation and abandonment, which the child never totally overcomes. Yet, if she acts in predictable ways, she can engender hope and trust in the infant. Separation helps shape the child's ego-identity; deprivation and the loss of the mother force the infant to distinguish himself or herself from her.
> - Foundations of trust and mistrust are established through the presence or absence of the parents' care and nurturing.
> - Parents guide the infant by the use of permission and prohibition. Infants tend to externalize their pain and discomfort by projecting them on to other objects.
> - The infant begins to gain control over the surrounding environment as he or she interacts with it.

Jacob's mind wandered all the way back to the beginning. He pictured the womblike Garden into which God had placed Adam Ha-Rishon, the first human being, and he could even feel the afterbirth that had covered Adam's body as he was placed there. Jacob could hear Adam's voice in his head as if he were forcing himself to remember every detail:

Content and Protected in the Garden of Our Infancy

dirt all over...
Genesis 2:7. The biblical text could be read to mean that Adam was created "as the dust."
called the Pishon...
Genesis 2:11.

The texture of the dirt all over my body was rough and scratchy, and it was difficult to rub off. I tried using the leaves that I had plucked from the large fig tree nearby, but they lacked sufficient moisture. It was only after I dipped the leaves in the water of the river called the Pishon that I was able to remove most of the grime. An indentation was left near the middle of my stomach, which remains to this day. Perhaps it was meant as a reminder of how I came into being: the product of heaven and earth.

breath God...
Genesis 2:7.

God created me from the soil of the earth, kneading it together and packing it as tight as possible. My body still aches from all the squeezing and pressing God had to do to shape me from the dirt. Yet, it was the breath God breathed into me that truly brought me to life. God's essence flowed into me. At the moment of my creation, when I was able to stand on my own two feet, I was at one with the Divine. Though created from the dust of the earth, like all subsequent offspring I was formed partly in the image of my Parent. It is true that I was created with two sets of characteristics, male and female, but like God I was one—a unity of different, perhaps complementary, parts.

two sets...
Genesis 1:26–27 and 5:1–2. Note the shift between the singular and plural objective particles (him...them).

In the time immediately following creation, all that I could focus on was the presence and nearness of God. It was as if God's spirit suffused all of creation and literally surrounded me. I could hardly tell the difference between myself and the Divine. God's presence was so total that in a sense I wasn't even aware of it.[1]

To my surprise, I was lifted up by a powerful gust of wind, which carried me to what I still think of as the most beautiful place in all the world. It is a place to which I long to return someday, a lush Garden in which every kind of vegetation grew: all kinds of fruit trees, multicolored flowers, and fragrant herbs, as well as bushes and plants of every size and shape.[2]

lush Garden...
It is called *Gan Eden*, the Garden of Eden, which is also a name for the world to come.

Adam was overwhelmed that this was the place God had prepared for him. By choosing Eden for Adam, God had displayed the love that most devoted parents have for their children in preparing the world for the arrival of their newborn.[3] God not only made sure that Adam and Eve had enough food to eat, but also created a space in which the first human beings would be happy and secure. Jacob heard Adam's voice, a voice full of contentment and pleasure:

food to eat...
Bereshit Rabbah 8:6. See also B.T. Shabbat 38a.

All that I need is right here in the Garden. I can eat whenever I am hungry. I can swim and bathe in the waters of the streams that irrigate the Garden. I can spend wonderful hours luxuriating in the beauty of the many plants, which thrill each of my five senses. I never feel bored. And I feel utterly safe here, since the Garden is hedged by huge trees, which prevent the animals outside from ever intruding upon me. The only animals I ever see are some harmless Garden snakes, who seem more interested in the fruit that falls from the trees.[4]

whenever I am hungry...
Genesis 2:8–15.

Adam was placed in a nursery of green in which to work and play to his heart's content amid the wonders of God's creation. Sheltered, cared for, and coddled, he was able to

fall into a deep...
Genesis 3:21.

curl up when he became tired and to fall into a deep, comforting sleep. Like all newborns, Adam was not afraid of ever being disturbed.

Becoming Aware of the Other

Adam was one with the earth, the *adamah*, and he was one with all creation. But he was also alone—solitary and single. As wonderful as his garden-like nursery was, God **it was not good...** knew that it was not good for Adam to be alone. If he could Genesis 2:18. relate to another creation similar to himself, he would better recognize who he was and the purpose of his life. He would also better understand his relationship with the Other in the universe, the Divine. Adam needed a mate, and Jacob remembered how it came to be.

God first brought several animals to Adam from outside the Garden so he could see that he was different from them. He was awed by their mammoth size and ferociousness. Yet, as he gazed at each of them he called them by **called them...** unique names, just as children do when they lie in a crib Genesis 2:20. and play with objects that seem to tower over them. Eventually, although the elephant and giraffe, the lion and the bear still made terrifying noises and threatened to devour Adam, they were no longer so frightening. After all, he had given them names to which they seemed to respond. It was almost as if he controlled them by calling them by name. He had power over all the animals, but it did not make him happy, and he expressed his sadness:

> It's amazing! How do the tigers and the anteaters and the raccoons all know that each of them is meant for its own kind?
> They seem attracted to one another. In a sense, they seem to be created for each other! But they are all different from me. Their bodies, the way they walk, the sounds they make, even the manner in which they relate to the other creations are very different.

Adam was lonely and longed to have a partner like himself.[5] And as he slept that night he dreamed of a creature like himself. He conceived of a being that would complement him—that would, in a sense, be a side of himself.[6] He awakened in the morning to find the very creature of which he had dreamed: a wo(man). And he cried out in amazement, "This one is like me: she is bone of my bones and flesh of my flesh." By finding his partner, Adam recognized even more the creative power of God, the One Who had created both of them.

partner like himself...
Genesis 2:18, 20.
Adam needed an *ezer kenegdo*, a fitting partner.

a side of himself...
Genesis 2:21–22.
Tzeila, "rib," also means "side."

she is bone...
Genesis 2:23.

The Need for Guidance and Limitations

But on his deathbed, Jacob recalled that Adam and Eve's joy in their nursery-like Garden was short-lived. They awakened to the reality of God's expectations of them. In the beginning, God indicated to them that all of creation was made for them, that the world was theirs: "Be fertile and increase, fill the earth and master it; and rule over the fish...the birds and all the living things that creep on the earth....I give to you every seed-bearing plant upon the earth, and every tree that has seed-bearing fruit...all the green plants for food." But when God placed Adam in the Garden, it was made clear that Adam could not simply enjoy the fruit of the Garden. Adam was given the responsibility of caring for it, and he wasn't pleased about this:

Be fertile and...
Genesis 1:28–30.

the responsibility of...
Genesis 2:15.

> It wasn't easy for me to tend to all the plants and trees. Just to keep track of which needed watering and which needed fertilizing was enough to make my head spin. And the workload was immense. There were so many trees, shrubs, and plants that I literally had to work from sunrise to sunset in order to keep up with it all. Do you think pruning, feeding, and replenishing a nursery full of an infinite variety of vegetation is easy? We hardly had any time to enjoy the Garden and all its beauty. But it got worse. I don't understand how

God, after saying that all of the trees in the Garden were given to us for food, could then command us not to eat the fruit of the tree in the middle of the Garden. What was so special about this Tree of Knowledge of Good and Evil to cause God to make up a special rule about it? It was clear that God had an important stake in setting this prohibition, since God—for the first time—not only commanded us not to do something, but also said that we would die if we ate the fruit.[7]

Tree of Knowledge...
Genesis 2:16-17.

As he remembered how God had placed before creation that which was both permitted and forbidden, Jacob understood that the Divine served as a paradigm for every parent who must walk a tightrope between permissiveness and discipline, extending unconditional love to their children while also having expectations for them. He had struggled throughout his life with this very tension.[8]

Yet, in presenting the human being with the permitted and the forbidden, God also gave Adam the gift of choice. This affirmed his freedom. The moment that Adam was told that he could not eat the fruit of the tree that was in the middle of the Garden was the instant that Adam became independent of God. Adam, like every child, now had the power to do what he wanted to do, irrespective of what had been told to him.[9]

Testing the Limits: The Beginning of Growth

Adam told Eve that God had made it clear that they could eat fruit from all the trees in the Garden of Eden except for the Tree of Knowledge of Good and Evil. Every day as Eve passed the tree she stared at it, for it seemed to have the most luscious, tasty, and beautiful fruit of all. She couldn't help herself; it was almost as if the tree were drawing her to it.

luscious, tasty...
Genesis 3:6.

One day, as she stood close to the tree, she heard a voice speaking to her. Or perhaps the voice came from within her. She looked around for Adam, but he wasn't in sight. The only thing she saw was a snake curled around a near-by bush.[10] The voice assured her that if she ate the delicious fruit, not only would she not die, but her eyes would be opened and she would gain wisdom. In her heart of hearts, she knew that she and Adam would be punished if they ate the fruit. She even thought that perhaps they shouldn't even touch the tree lest they be drawn to the tempting fruit.

eyes would be opened...
Genesis 3:5–6.

even touch...
Genesis 3:3.

But the voice was very compelling. At that moment, she saw the serpent move toward the tree and touch the base of its trunk. Nothing happened to it. This only added to Eve's confusion as she struggled to make sense of her conflicting impulses.[11]

The first seeds of doubt about God's command had already taken root. Did God really say, "You shall eat of any tree of the Garden?" Perhaps it *was* permissible to eat the fruit of the tree in the middle of the Garden, since God had initially said that *all* the trees and vegetation were available for consumption. Jacob remembered that he had heard not only that the fruit was beautiful to look at and had a fantastic aroma, but that anyone who ate it would be wise like God.

Eve and Adam were like all children who begin to doubt their parents' rules while striving to be like them.[12] They had to test just how far they could assert themselves while they were learning about their own power. Jacob did not find this surprising at all, since they were created in the image of their parent, God, who is unique and all-powerful.[13]

And so Eve extended her hand toward one of the limbs. Ever so delicately, she removed a piece of fruit, trying not to disturb the branch at all—as if that would guarantee that God would not realize what she had done. She smiled as

[27]

she enjoyed the delicious fruit, and she couldn't wait to share it with Adam.

And Their Eyes Were Opened;
Recognizing the Other in Us

Eve soon found Adam, and the two of them now ate the fruit. But they both sensed that something had changed. From the first moment they had gazed at each other, they knew that they were similar to each other and very different from all the other creatures they had seen lurking outside the Garden. Though in many respects they were absolutely naive as they witnessed each other's nakedness, now they saw each other through different eyes. Eve couldn't take her eyes off Adam, but she didn't want to be caught staring at him.[14]

> I can't believe how wonderful it is that our bodies seem to match; the parts complement each other. I wonder if Adam's body is as sensitive to touch as mine seems to be. I want to caress him and warm him with my body.

Eve was ashamed to think such thoughts and looked for something with which to cover herself. Adam suggested they use fig leaves, remembering how he had tried to clean himself with these leaves after his own creation. Eve ran and brought back a handful of leaves, which she quickly sewed together into cloths to cover the parts of their bodies that represented their uniqueness.

Shame occurs when someone is totally exposed and conscious of someone else's gaze. Before eating the fruit of the Tree of Knowledge, Adam and Eve had no self-consciousness.[15] They did not fully know each other; in a way, they did not even know themselves. Only when they became totally visible to each other did they truly

they were similar... based on Genesis 2:23.

each other's nakedness... Genesis 2:25.

comprehend who they were. Only when they could share the totality of their being with each other could Adam and Eve develop their full individuality.[16] They had finally become the helpmate for each other that God had spoken about by proclaiming, "It is not good for the human being to be alone; I will find a fitting helper for him."

It is not good...
Genesis 2:18.

Hiding from Responsibility

The embarrassment that Eve and Adam felt toward each other because of their nakedness did not compare to the shame they felt before God. Jacob could still feel their terror as they sensed God's presence in the Garden. Like all young children, Adam and Eve were more acutely aware of their Parent when they did something wrong.

sensed God's presence...
Genesis 3:8.

The irony, of course, was that God was always present, but they could not be sure of that, since they had not seen God for what seemed to be an eternity. Their relationship to God was like a game of hide-and-seek or peek-a-boo—games that teach all infants not only basic trust but also that they can survive independently of their parents. God seemed to disappear—and not return. While God "was gone" they continued to live. As a result of the "game," Adam and Eve probably felt a greater sense of themselves and their own needs and power.

Yet, having tasted of the fruit of the Tree of Knowledge of Good and Evil, the first man and woman instinctively tried to hide among the largest trees.[17] Suddenly, a booming voice pierced through the Garden and seemed to reverberate in their own heads: "Where are you?" The pair crouched down and didn't know what to do.

Do you think we should respond? The Divine is bound to find us. God probably knows where we are, anyway! We know that was not what God was asking: it was a question of what we have done.

[29]

Adam finally stammered to God:

I...I mean we heard You moving through the Garden...and...well...we were afraid because we were naked, so we hid.

we were naked...
Genesis 3:10.

Eve thought to herself:

We're not naked anymore: We're now covered with the fig leaves that I sewed together for us. But perhaps we are naked in God's eyes—or maybe in our own eyes—because of what we did, and we tried to avoid God's anger, just as the serpent here slithers away when danger approaches.[18]

were naked...
Genesis 3:11.

Adam replied...
Genesis 3:11–13.

When God asked who told them that they were naked, or whether they had gained such knowledge by eating from the tree that was forbidden to them, Adam replied, "The woman made me do it," and Eve claimed, "The serpent duped me." Jacob could only imagine whom the serpent would blame!

It was so typically childlike to cast blame on others and not take responsibility for what they had done. It was much easier for Adam and Eve to say that the snake had been culpable, to project onto him their own desire (even if it was an unconscious desire) for independence and power, which could be attained by eating the fruit of the Tree of Knowledge of Good and Evil.

Leaving the Garden—the Womb

Jacob knew that God had searched through the Garden for Adam and Eve. Finally, God asked, "*Aiyeka*," "Where are you?" Things seemed to have changed so much. God could no longer be sure of the creatures of creation, asking them not so much "where they were" but rather "who they were." It was almost as if the Divine, like all parents, no longer completely knew the very creatures that God had

God asked...
Genesis 3:8–9.

produced. God was dealing with growing progeny, who were developing personalities and wills of their own. As Adam and Eve began to assert their independence from the Divine, perhaps God also understood that it was time to withdraw from them. Parents also consciously contract somewhat, so they can give their children the space they need to fully develop.[19]

But it is not easy for parents—or for God—to withdraw. This usually is done with great ambivalence. On one hand, God wanted them to live and flourish, and as a result they were not immediately stricken with death when the Divine realized that they had disobeyed the commandment against eating from the tree. Yet, God punished them for asserting their own independence. Doing this showed them the difficulty of childbearing and childrearing: "I shall make most severe your pain in childbearing; in pain you shall bring children into the world." God realized that Adam and Eve had to leave the Garden where they had been protected, since they could not grow in the confines of the womb. This is no different from children's need to leave the safety of their parents' house. However, as God was about to banish them, God reacted like every loving parent:

> Wait! Don't go so fast. You cannot go like that: Without garments to protect you, you will not survive outside the Garden. The cold can be very biting; thorns and branches will tear at your skin; animals may sting or scratch or bite you. You have no idea what you will encounter out there. Please, put on these coverings, which I have sewn together from skins that the serpents have shed. In this way, I will be with you, protecting you at every step.[20]

As God breathed in, Eden contracted like a womb and expelled Adam and Eve into the world.[21] They could never return to the place where everything that was necessary for

not immediately stricken…
In Genesis 2:17, God said, "As soon as you eat of [the fruit], you will die."
"I shall make…"
Genesis 3:16.

from skins…
Genesis 3:21.

life had been provided. But the irony was that their lives were only now really beginning. By leaving the Garden, they took their first steps toward determining who they were, their first steps toward choosing freely their own path in the world.[22]

After taking a few steps, Adam turned to gaze at the place where he and Eve had felt at one with the Divine—the place where he had been secure and at peace. As he turned, something in him wanted to run back, almost as if he had left a part of himself there. One part of him, indeed, would always dream of that place of his infancy and of the time that was so simple, so clear, so certain.

Cherubim...
Genesis 3:24.

But there was no going back. Cherubim and a fiery sword prevented Adam and Eve from returning. They were destined to live in exile outside the Garden, in a place where creativity and hope would always have to battle limitation and anxiety. At best, all they could carry with them was the memory of Eden. This became their road map for an eventual return. The garden of their infancy became their dream of utopia and fulfillment.[23]

Adam and Eve now began their journey to the wholeness and completeness they had known in the Garden. Much later, Jacob would long for this wholeness his entire life. As Adam and Eve remembered deep in their psyches the time when they were at one with God in the all-enveloping womb of Eden, they were already on their way back to the Divine, Whom they would encounter as adults in the garden of their maturity.[24]

CHAPTER TWO

CAIN AND ABEL

Early Childhood

Erik Erikson: Stage Two
Autonomy vs. Shame and Doubt

- The child's willpower is reflected in the determination to exercise free choice as well as self-restraint. The child's free will encounters social boundaries, and he or she needs to learn to balance freedom of self-expression with cooperation and restraint.
- The child has a sense of possessiveness; autonomy is often expressed in keeping other rivals out. This can lead to jealous rage, which is often directed at siblings.
- Shame and doubt involve being aware of another side of the self, which others do not see. The child needs to control that side, which can be impulsive, emotional, aggressive, and libidinal. The challenge is to exert self-control without losing self-esteem.
- The parent needs to help the child see the limits to his or her power and learn how to control emotions. The child needs the parent's approval and help, but also often resists parental help in an attempt to assert independence.
- The child must learn that there are consequences to his or her actions, and also learn how to avoid punishment.

From somewhere deep inside of him, Jacob called forth the ancestral memory of leaving the Garden and the fear and excitement that Adam and Eve had experienced as they learned to navigate the world beyond Paradise. In the beginning, everything they needed had been provided for them; now they had to work to ensure their survival. The fruit of the trees of the Garden was no longer available for the picking; they would have to till the soil to produce their food. As their Divine Parent slowly receded into the background they had to step up to a sense of their own responsibility.[1]

Farmer and Shepherd: Dependence upon the Other

It was no coincidence, then, that the only thing Jacob could remember about the children of Adam and Eve, aside from their birth, was that Cain had become a farmer, while Abel had become a shepherd. He could not recall anything else about them, but he knew that they had provided food for their family. But surely the livelihoods they had adopted could tell Jacob something about who Cain and Abel were and what was important to them. All he had to do was to listen to their voices. Cain, for instance, wanted to make his father proud of him:

Cain had become...
Genesis 4:2.

> All I wanted was to please our father, but I did not realize how difficult it would be. Some children follow in their parents' footsteps. I thought it would give him great pleasure if I became a farmer like him. We could work together and spend more time together, and he would teach me all that he knew about cultivating the land, which he had learned while living in the Garden. Surely, this would draw us closer. Only in passing had my father mentioned the curse that God had placed upon the land, making it difficult to grow anything. And although I knew how hard he worked every day, he rarely ever complained. So I thought he actually enjoyed

curse that God...
Genesis 3:17.

working the land. On the other hand, my brother Abel never had any interest in farming. He was always out in the fields with the sheep and seemed to prefer the solitude. He was even convinced that God preferred that we not work the land, since it had been cursed many years before.[2] I wonder if he ever told our father how he felt.

Abel and I couldn't have been more different. After all, what do a shepherd and farmer have in common?[3] Yet, for all our differences, we needed each other, since we could never have survived by ourselves. We gave to each other the food that we produced; he enjoyed my fruits and vegetables; I savored the lamb and veal he provided. He also gave me some animal skins and wool, which were so necessary in the changing weather outside the Garden (something our parents had never worried about in Paradise).[4] And I must confess that as we walked together every morning, Abel toward his flocks and I toward the fields that I would plough and till, we knew that even though we were utterly different, we were tied to each other forever.

walked together...
Sefer ha-Yashar,
Chapter 1.

Pleasing Our Parents By Giving of Ourselves

Jacob was astounded by how much he remembered about Cain and Abel. Perhaps it was because he, like Cain, had a brother whom he both loved and hated. He could not totally understand what Cain had felt, since he was the younger sibling. Yet, as he lay in his tent waiting for Joseph to arrive with his two sons he wondered why the same struggles seemed to repeat generation after generation in every family, and especially why children needed to give of themselves to their parents in the hope of gaining favor with them and receiving a blessing. Remarkably, children didn't have to be told to do this: Wanting to please their parents was a natural impulse.

One day, in the fall, after harvesting the late fruit, Cain was dividing the produce; setting some aside for his parents, some for his brother, and some for himself. But it occurred to him for the first time that he had never set aside a portion of what he had grown as a thanksgiving offering to God. He ruminated about why he had not thought of this before:

Perhaps it is because I never saw my father bring to God an offering of the food that he produced. During all the years that he farmed the land, I never once saw him build an altar and sacrifice any fruits or vegetables to God. And he never mentioned that God commanded him to make such an offering. Had he mentioned this, I would have known that it was expected of me, too.

Yet, I knew in my heart that it was the right thing to do. But what should I bring? How should I know which fruits and vegetables to set aside for God? Perhaps it does not matter; all that is important is to show God that I am grateful that we can enjoy the food we have brought forth from the earth.

sacrificed the produce...
Genesis 4:3. Though the Bible does not mention that Cain built an altar, the rabbis do in several sources, e.g., Pirkei d'Rabbi Eliezer, Chapter 31.
God did not notice...
Genesis 4:4–5.
brought the finest...
Genesis 4:4.
got furious...
Genesis 4:5.

And so Cain took some produce from the three piles he had set aside and placed it upon a small altar that he had built. He then sacrificed the produce to God. Cain's offering was totally voluntary, but he did not take the time to choose the best fruits and vegetables. He simply picked them indiscriminately from the three piles.[5]

When God did not notice Cain's offering, Cain became distraught. Making the situation worse was that Abel, who had witnessed the entire scene, immediately brought the finest of the firstborn of his flock and placed them on the altar that Cain had built.[6] When God accepted Abel's offering, Cain felt rejected and got furious.

Projecting Rejection onto the Other

Cain was confused and deflated, and couldn't understand what had happened to him:

Why would God reject the offering I gave with a full heart? And why would He accept the offering from my brother?[7] I wanted to sacrifice some of my fruits and vegetables to show my gratitude to the Creator who let me produce a successful crop. It was my idea to bring sacrifices to God. And what is worse, Abel realized that he should make a sacrifice only after I had made mine! I thought that this was a world of goodness and justice, but I now see that good deeds bear no fruit. I see that God's rule is arbitrary. If not, then why would my sacrifice be rejected and Abel's accepted? There is no justice in the world.

Abel realized...
Based on Genesis 4:4: "And Abel, he also brought."
a world of goodness...
The Palestinian Targum and Midrash Aggadah to Genesis 4:8ff.

From Cain's point of view, what he experienced had nothing to do with his actions. His intention was pure, but if God rejected the offering that he had produced with the sweat of his brow, it was because God was not just. Like every young child, Cain had to blame someone. But the Divine Parent was not the only available object upon which Cain could blame his rejection. There was also Abel, whose sacrifice had been accepted.

For the first time, Cain now perceived the otherness of Abel in a most acute way.[8] Although it was inevitable that Cain, like all siblings, would experience a sense of inequality simply because he had a brother, the pain was sharper because he felt that his younger brother had encroached upon his favored position as the firstborn. In truth, this was a battle for their Divine Parent's favor and recognition, and the sacrifices were the field upon which the competition between the two was played out. What transpired between Cain and Abel was as much a part of the human psyche as it was a thread of the fabric of the sibling relationship: defending one's turf. And it eventually led to the raw aggression that came from Cain.[9]

Spelling out Consequences: Will the Child Listen?

Why are you distressed...
Genesis 4:7.

Sensing Cain's pain, God asked, "Why are you distressed? Why is your face fallen? Surely if you do right, there is uplift. But if you do not do right, sin crouches at the door; its urge is upon you, yet you have the capacity to control it." God, like most parents, was trying to tell Cain to control his emotions, and that his actions have consequences. But Cain was stunned and confused by what he heard from God. Unlike Adam and Eve, to whom God had spelled out the prohibitions to which they were subject, and their punishment if they disobeyed, Cain was not sure what God meant.[10] So Cain just shook his head as he thought to himself:

> Why doesn't God understand how I feel? I brought my fruits and God didn't even notice them, while He accepted the sheep that Abel offered. Now God says that if I had brought the right offering, my fruit would have been accepted! I can't believe this. Maybe God is challenging me by saying that no matter what has happened, it will be better if I can control my reaction and not let it eat away at me.[11] Either way, God had no idea how I felt. If God did, why would I have been asked why I was so upset in the first place?

Cain could not bring himself to respond to the Divine. Even though God, like most parents, was trying to help Cain understand his predicament and learn from it, Cain chose to remain silent. By doing so, he let his pain fester and turn to rage. But finding the words to express feelings is difficult for most children to do, just as it was difficult for Cain to do—especially in the face of a strong, demanding parent, even if the parent seems to entreat the child to respond.[12] To express feelings to a parent, especially if they involve deep-seated anger, is too daunting even for the most precocious child. It is much easier to take out those feelings on someone who is weaker and more available. It is especially easier to take them out on a younger sibling. This is even more true if the brother or sister helped trigger the events that prompted the sore feelings in the first place.[13]

Reaching out to Our Sibling: The Need for a Response

Since Adam and Eve were not there for him, and since Cain could not tell God how he felt, the only one left to speak to was his brother, Abel. He was not sure what he would say to Abel, but he knew that he would say something. So as they were walking together out to the fields the next day, Cain found himself rehearsing what he would say:[14]

walking together... Sefer ha-Yashar, Chapter 1.

> I can't believe that you did this to me! How could you wait until the very moment when my offering was rejected to bring forth your sheep? You saw what happened. You knew that God must have preferred the animal sacrifices, and you also knew there was no way I could please God. Not only don't I understand why my fruit was not as acceptable as your animals, but I can't comprehend what drove you to hurt me.
>
> But how can I blame Abel? What did he do to hurt me? Nothing. It wasn't his fault that I was treated like this. Perhaps he can simply explain what happened. Maybe in my zeal to please, I missed something. Maybe I should have known what God wanted.
>
> Abel, can you make some sense out of all this for me? Tell me what happened. Speak to me, please.[15]

As they walked along Cain struggled to find the right words to express how he felt. But he vacillated so much between anger and betrayal, and rejection and isolation, that the words simply would not come out.

would not come out...
Genesis 4:8 states, "Cain said to his brother Abel," but the words are missing.[16]

Perhaps all Cain needed was some indication from Abel that he understood the pain that he was going through. But it isn't always easy to bare one's soul to a sibling, especially if he or she has something to do with the pain we are experiencing.

it had taken him and Esau...
See their reconciliation in Genesis, Chapter 33.

Jacob knew how difficult that could be. After all, it had taken him and Esau more than twenty years after he stole the birthright until they finally spoke directly to each other, and even then Esau could not bring himself to express the rejection that he had felt. Jacob could easily imagine what Cain was thinking:

> Why doesn't he say something? He knows how hurt I've been; he could see it on my face. How could he remain silent and not show some sign of compassion? Is he so smug that he doesn't care how I feel? Or is he just oblivious to me and my feelings? Whatever the reason, I cannot take his silence.

Abel's lack of response must have been very difficult for Cain, and it surely intensified his feelings. If only Abel could have comforted him, or at least put forth some gesture to show his concern for his brother, then perhaps Cain would have been mollified. But Abel was just not there for him.[17] It was as if he were walking alone in the field.

An Outburst of Anger:
The Struggle to Control Emotions

Cain felt alone in the world—abandoned by his parents, rejected and chastised by God, ignored by his brother. There was no one to whom he could turn who would understand what he was going through. As they walked, Cain sensed his anger rising. He glared at Abel, who didn't even notice that he was upset. This only exacerbated Cain's feelings. All he could think about was how unfair this was and how smug Abel seemed to be. Cain's favored position as firstborn had clearly been usurped, and he was convinced that his life would never be the same again.

If only Cain had been able to really hear God's words to him: "If you do right, there is uplift. But if you do not do right, sin crouches at the door; its urge is upon you, yet you have the capacity to control it." In essence, God told Cain that he had the ability to respond to what happened in a reasonable manner. This is what every concerned, responsible parent does who senses a child's anger. Doing this would help Cain lift himself out of his emotional tailspin.[18] If, however, he let his emotions get the best of him, the situation would only get worse. Like all children, Cain needed to maintain some degree of self-control and learn how to sublimate his feelings effectively.

If you do right...
Genesis 4:7.

But that is too much to ask of most children, especially when they are overcome by such primal, raw instincts as was Cain. His response came from somewhere deep inside of him. Threatened by Abel and sensing that he had lost his dominant position, he could not resist the fury that was welling up from the core of his being—a fury that, as God had anticipated, Cain could not control. It was simply too early in his emotional development for him to do this.[19]

As Jacob reflected upon Cain he recalled his own brother, Esau. Had he not fled, Esau probably would have killed him when he stole the blessing and usurped Esau's position as firstborn. Abel would not be as fortunate.

would have killed him...
See Genesis 27:31–46.

If only Cain had possessed a sense of the consequences of his actions. But that can only develop as a person grows and matures. In one moment, Cain's frustration, pain, and rejection turned, in a childlike fashion, into brute hostility, and he lashed out at Abel. Perhaps he did not intend to kill his brother, but he surely knew what killing was, having seen Abel sacrifice animals from his flock to God. How ironic it was that by killing his brother, Cain was emulating Abel's actions! Abel was Cain's sacrifice, and Abel was surely more beloved in God's eyes than the fruit that Cain had brought earlier.

Facing the Consequences of Our Actions

Where is...
Genesis 4:9.

Jacob now heard the accusatory words that God had spoken to Cain as if they had been meant for him: "Where is your brother?" What have you done to him? How could you do something so terrible? Having duped Esau out of his birthright and stolen the blessing of the firstborn, he fled to Haran to escape his brother's wrath. By the time he returned to Canaan more than twenty years later, his brother seemed to have forgotten what had transpired and never vented any of his anger at Jacob. Unlike Cain, Jacob never had to respond to God's challenge regarding his responsibility.

The meaning of God's question to Cain was absolutely clear, since God knew where Abel was: lying in the earth not far from where Cain was standing. The Divine was now simply asking Cain what he had done. Jacob was not sure if he would have responded differently from the way Cain did:

I did not know that I am my brother's keeper.[20] No one explained to me what was expected of me; I had no notion of my obligation to Abel, let alone to God. What is worse, You, God, made us the way we are: You created us with all our flaws. We are not perfect. We are bound to fail. And now you demand a full account from me!

You created us...
Cain's remarks are based on Midrash Tanhuma ha-Nidpas Bereshit 9.

But there is more. You are the keeper and preserver of all things, yet you even let me kill my brother. Why didn't you stop me? You had the power to do that at any moment.

Besides, if you had accepted my offering as you did his, I would have had no reason to envy him. I would not have harmed him. You are the real murderer.[21]

Cain sounded like most young children who do not know what it means to take responsibility for their actions. The claim of ignorance—"I don't know"—typifies their responses. The denial of their own culpability, even in the face of glaring evidence ("What have you done? Your brother's blood cries out to Me from the ground") is astonishing. How can it be so easy to be caught with your hand in the cookie jar and still deny your guilt?[22]

> **What have you done...** Genesis 4:10.

All children must learn that there are direct consequences to their actions. God, as parent figure, conveyed that immediately to Cain: "Therefore, you shall be more cursed than the ground, which opened its mouth to receive your brother's blood from your hand. If you till it, it shall no longer yield its strength to you. You shall become a ceaseless wanderer on earth." By killing Abel, Cain would suffer. He was a farmer and was banished from the very thing that defined his existence: the land. He lost a significant part of himself; his punishment was self-alienation. The farmer now became the wanderer. Little did Cain know that by injuring Abel he would be injuring—perhaps even killing—a part of himself.[23]

> **Therefore, you shall be...** Genesis 4:11–12.

But the impact of Cain's actions extended beyond himself. While it is almost impossible for children to fathom the extent of the harm and pain that their actions can cause, their parent is still obliged to underscore just that message, in the hope that it will eventually be internalized as the child matures.

Then [God] said:

What have you done? All the potential future progeny of your brother, Abel, cry out to Me from the ground. Don't you understand that you have obliterated his entire line by taking

> **Then [God] said...** Based on Genesis 4:10, in which the word "blood" is written in the plural, *demei achicha* (brother's bloods).

[43]

his life? The blood you have spilled is the life force of innumerable future generations that will not be born.

Learning to Take Responsibility

This was not the first time that God had spoken to Cain and tried to show him what he had done wrong. As do most parents, God first asked Cain in a rather oblique way to consider why his offering was not accepted: "Why are you distressed and why is your face fallen? Surely, if you do right, there is uplift, but if you do not do right..." But Cain did not respond to God. If only he had been able to truly hear God's words, or at least to somehow verbalize his feelings, perhaps Abel's death could have been avoided. But after Abel's murder, God confronted Cain directly, challenging him to acknowledge what he had done: "Where is Abel, your brother?" Cain was not ready to accept responsibility for his actions, but he did answer God. And his words, "Am I my brother's keeper" tacitly recognized that there is a higher moral authority to Whom all human beings must respond, just as children learn this lesson about their parents.[24] Cain's lesson was this: There is a force in the world that has a moral claim on us, and we cannot hide from God as Adam did in the Garden, as children cower upon hearing the demanding voice of their parent. Cain recognized and acknowledged *Anochi*, the commanding presence of God, which demands accountability, even though he still did not have the inner strength to admit his own guilt.[25]

But God was persistent. Following Cain's insistence that he was not responsible for his brother, God gave Cain one final chance: "What have you done? Your brother's blood cries out to Me from the ground!" But Cain did not respond, and God immediately informed him of his

Why are you distressed...
Genesis 4:6–7.

Where is Abel...
Genesis 4:9.

What have you done...
Genesis 4:10.

punishment: to be cut off from the earth and to wander forever.

Facing the harsh punishment (the loss of his basic identity as a farmer), and realizing his new vulnerability—anyone who met him might kill him—a new Cain emerged. No longer arrogant, he was contrite and accepted responsibility for what he had done:[26]

> My sin is too great for me to bear alone.[27] God, You bear the burden of the entire world, yet my sin You cannot bear? You Yourself have written, "Who is a God like unto You that bears iniquity and forgives transgression (Micah 7:18)?" Please, pardon my iniquity for it is great![28]

the loss of his basic... Based on Genesis 4:14.

That Cain had matured was apparent. Not only did he confess his sin, but also he understood that he could not survive on his own. By crying out "My sin is too great to bear," he demonstrated that he needed God to help him.[29] Cain was like most children who learn, no matter how uncomfortable it makes them, that they lack the ability to control their lives totally by themselves. They do need to rely on others. Thus, a humble Cain said:

> Since You have banished me this day from the soil, I must avoid your Presence. But how can I live without You? I cannot possibly survive alone in the world. How can you expect me to pick up and leave the place that I have known all of my life, and venture out into the world? I will be totally unprotected and vulnerable. Anyone who meets me may kill me! Please, promise me that Your presence will never abandon me, though I am cut off from the very basis of my life—the soil.

Since You have... Genesis 4:14.

Anyone who meets me... Genesis 4:14.

The Mark on Cain

Cain was no different from most children. He needed to know that his parents were still there for him, that God's presence was still very much evident. Indeed, Cain's recognition of his sin did propitiate God. When he finally uttered the words, "My sin is too great to bear," God forgave him.[30] And even though Cain was banished from the soil and became a wanderer looking for sustenance, God responded to his plight by pledging to protect him: "I promise, if anyone kills Cain, seven-fold vengeance shall be taken on him." God seemed to have changed His attitude toward Cain, and the tone of God's remarks was palpably different from the accusatory nature of the prior challenge to Cain to tell God where Abel was. God, the parent figure, was now protective of Cain. Cain no longer experienced the wrath of God's justice, but rather enjoyed God's compassion:[31]

I promise...
Genesis 4:15.

> Since anyone who will encounter Cain will think that he is alone and unprotected, I must ensure his safety by placing an identifying mark upon him, which will signify that he is still under My protection. Just as I placed the rainbow in the sky as a sign that I had not abandoned humanity following the Flood, so, too, Cain shall bear a sign of the covenant and My continuing relationship with him.[32]

left God's presence...
Based on
Genesis 4:16.

Even though Cain thought that he had left God's presence, he carried God with him. And although God originally declared that Cain would ceaselessly wander the earth, Cain could now settle in the Land of Nod, east of Eden.[33]

CHAPTER THREE

NOAH

Play Age

> ### Erik Erikson: Stage Three
> ### Initiative vs. Guilt
>
> - Initiative added to autonomy allows the child to undertake a plan to achieve a task. The child then possesses the courage to envision and pursue valued, tangible goals, and to move into the unknown and follow his or her curiosity.
> - Sometimes there is guilt over the targeted goals, since they may rival others' goals.
> - Passivity is the polar opposite of initiative. It is the acceptance of what is and the failure to even attempt to accomplish something.
> - The child is also ready to accept a sense of moral responsibility: conscience regulates initiative. He or she is eager to act cooperatively with others to accomplish a task. This sometimes leads to a conflict between unbounded initiative and inhibition, between individualism and accepted rules of social behavior.
> - There is a strong affection for home and family, but also the desire to venture beyond these institutions. There is also a fluctuation between dependence and independence, between maturity and antisocial behavior. The child can be affectionate but also quarrelsome and argumentative.

Lying on his bed, Jacob saw the generations after Cain quickly pass before his eyes. After Abel's death, Adam and Eve had another son, Seth, who was an affirmation to them of the future of the human race. Having fathered twelve sons, Jacob knew how children represent the hope for the future and how they specifically embodied the future of his people, Israel.

Adam and Eve had...
Genesis 4:25.

Now, ten generations after Adam and Eve and their banishment from the Garden, Jacob recalled that Lamech had fathered Noah, who would relieve human beings from their toil because the soil they worked had been cursed by God. Noah's name meant "rest" or "relief."

Noah, who would relieve...
Based on
Genesis 5:29.

My father Lamech called me Noah because I am supposed to bring relief to humankind from the harshness and pain of our lives.[1] According to the stories handed down, it wasn't always like this.

Our earliest ancestors lived in a magical garden in which all the necessities of life were provided in abundance. Without our taking a spade to the ground, the earth brought forth lush vegetation and fruits and vegetables of all kinds. But when the first human beings ate from one of the trees in the Garden that had been forbidden them, they were banished from the Garden. Now, they and all their progeny had to work the land with the sweat of the brow to provide food for themselves. Because they ate from the forbidden tree, the earth was cursed, and they experienced continual hardship.

the earth was cursed...
Genesis 3:17.

My father's hope was that my actions would relieve the curse of past generations, which had been in effect from the time that Adam and Eve left the Garden. I would be the one to bring comfort to all humankind.[2]

But Lamech's optimism did not come to fruition.

The Disappointed Parent Lashes Out

Although God had remarked "Behold, it is very good" after creating Adam and completing all of creation itself, much had changed. As human beings grew, God was quick to recognize their essential nature: "The Lord saw how great was humankind's wickedness...and how every plan devised by them was evil all the time."

Behold, it is very good...
Genesis 1:31.

The Lord saw...
Genesis 6:5.

Many parents' euphoria when a child is born quickly gives way to frustration and even disappointment. Inexplicably, their little angel develops into a terror in a matter of a few short years! So God said:

> I simply cannot believe what has happened. I don't understand it at all. How could it be? Had I known what human beings would be like, I might not have created them in the first place. I thought that as a result of their punishment for eating the fruit of the Tree of Knowledge of Good and Evil, they would learn and mature.
>
> I thoroughly regret having created humans on the earth. My heart is very sad.[3]

regret having created...
Based on Genesis 6:6.

God could not differentiate between a child's actions and his or her nature,[4] and saw humanity, which was now in its infancy, as utterly hopeless and degenerate.[5] And like most parents who cannot understand and tolerate their young child's disturbing behavior, God lashed out fiercely and almost indiscriminately:

> I will blot out from the earth the human being whom I created and the beasts, the creeping things and the birds of the sky. For I regret that I made them.

I will blot out...
Genesis 6:7.

A Child Can Mitigate a Parent's Anger

But all it takes is one child who listens and responds to the parent—one child who is obedient—to mollify the parent in some way. Such a child was Noah, for he found favor in God's eyes. Though God was sure that "all flesh had corrupted its ways on the earth" and was ready to "make an end of all flesh because the earth was filled with lawlessness because of them," Noah would bring God comfort.[6] His nature and his actions would justify some hope for the future.

an end of all flesh...
Genesis 6:12–13.

If I needed a reason to preserve the existence of humankind on the earth, Noah would be it. While the entire earth is filled with corruption and lawlessness, Noah, by contrast, is a righteous person. In this generation, his actions stand out and set him apart. Although he will father three sons, his legacy will be his righteous behavior.[7]

the entire earth...
Based on Genesis 6:11–12.
In this generation...
Based on Genesis 6:9–10.

But what shall I do? Except for Noah, all humankind is corrupt and deserves to die. How can I allow these lawless creatures to go unpunished just because Noah is righteous? So...I must destroy all the flesh under the sky in which there is life; everything on earth shall perish. But I will keep My covenant with Noah. Only he will walk with Me.

I must destroy...
Genesis 6:17–18, as well Genesis 6:9, which states that "Noah walked with God."
Make for yourself...
Genesis 6:14,18–19.

Noah, I have decided to put an end to all flesh, for the earth is filled with corruption.... Make for yourself an ark of gopher wood...and enter the ark with your sons, your wife, and your sons' wives. And of all that lives, of all flesh, you shall take two of each into the ark to keep alive with you.

Noah followed God's commands to the letter; every detail was planned and carried out with precision and zeal. Noah invested himself totally in the project, showing his dedication and his initiative.[8] Finally, the ark was built and Noah, his family, and an array of animals were all saved, just as God had predicted.

The flood covered the earth for one hundred and fifty days, blotting out all life until the waters began to recede. To discover if the water had receded enough so he could exit from the ark, Noah showed initiative and insight. At first, he sent out a raven. When the raven did not return, he sent out a dove. When it returned carrying an olive leaf in its bill, Noah knew that vegetation was growing again. But when the dove did not return at all to the ark, Noah realized that much of the earth had dried and that he and his family and all the creatures could exit from their haven. By this, Noah showed his developing maturity: He conceived of a well-thought-out plan to test the waters, and he carried it out to perfection.

he sent out a raven... Based on Genesis 8:7–12.

The Child Builds an Ark for Himself

Recalling the story of the ark and the flood, Jacob identified with Noah. It was as if they were the same personality. Jacob knew about making plans and carrying them out to help guarantee the future. He also knew about being a young child and seeing oneself singled out for blessing, as was Noah.

making plans... See Genesis 25:27–34 and Genesis 27, in which Jacob usurps the birthright and the blessing of the firstborn.

The Lord said to Noah, "Go into the ark…for you alone have I found righteous before Me in this generation." And Noah believed it. When God commanded him to "make for yourself an ark," he took it literally. He did just as God commanded, all the while berating those around him:[9]

The Lord said... Genesis 7:1.

make for yourself... Genesis 6:14.

> God intends to bring a flood upon the world. You had years to repent and did not. You saw me making the ark, yet never once did you retreat from your evil ways. Yes, God instructed me, and me alone, to build this ark so that I and my wife and my children can escape the devastation that will surely come. The future of the world will come through my line.[10]

Noah, of course, felt justified in feeling the way he did, since he believed that only he was worthy to carry on the covenant with God. God had told him that in no uncertain

**I am about to
bring...**
Genesis 6:17–18.

terms: "I am about to bring a flood…to destroy all flesh under the sun…. But I will establish my covenant with you." As a result, as with an immature child, Noah's ego prevented him from caring about others. Had he cared for those outside of his family, he might have argued with God to save humanity. But all he did was build an ark for himself and his family.

Noah saw the world through the narrow prism of his own life and his own needs. He was concerned only about himself—a trait evident in most young children.[11] He seemed to show a lack of compassion for all the rest of humanity, which was about to be destroyed. All that mattered to him was that the ark would guarantee his survival and that of his household.[12] So he built the ark, and as a result, only he and his family were left when the waters subsided. They were the sole remnant of the antediluvian world of Adam and Eve, and Cain and Abel.

**only he and his
family were left...**
Genesis 7:24.

Receiving a Parent's Blessing

Noah felt safe in the ark, despite the chaos and ferocity of the flood outside. It was a sanctuary: warm, dry, and secure no matter how terrible the winds and rain raged. He saw himself as an obedient child who is loved and protected by his or her merciful parent.[13]

God was not surprised by Noah's selfishness. After all, ever since Adam and Eve's behavior in the Garden of Eden, God had known that human nature was less than perfect. Even more to the point, God recognized that the ways of humankind had been evil from their earliest days, and it was that knowledge that persuaded the Divine to destroy every living being.

the ways...
Based on
Genesis 8:21.

Yet, like most parents, God could be easily appeased by His progeny. So when Noah, after leaving the ark, erected an altar to the Lord, offering every clean type of animal

erected an altar...
Genesis 8:20–21.

and fowl as a way to acknowledge his dependence upon God, God was mollified. The aroma of the sacrifices pleased God, Who resolved never to destroy the earth again and, by blessing Noah and his sons, recalled when Adam had also been blessed shortly after his creation:

blessing Noah...
Genesis 9:1. See also
Genesis 1:28–29.

How shall I communicate to Noah just how important he is to Me? Surely, he is like Adam at the moment of his creation. After all, isn't it as though the Flood had returned the world to a state of chaos, as it was before the Creation itself? The world has been returned to Tohu ["void"] and Noah has been reborn, sent forth from the womb-like ark, which had floated on the amniotic waters of the flood. He will now repopulate the earth.

As I commanded Adam, I say to you, Noah, and to your sons: "Be fruitful and increase, and fill the earth. And the fear...of you shall be upon all the beasts of the earth and upon all the birds of the sky...and upon all the fish of the sea; they are given over to your hand. Every creature that lives shall be yours to eat; as with green grasses, I give all these to you."[14]

But I shall grant you, Noah, a special gift that I did not give Adam. I shall make a covenant with you and your descendants, a covenant which declares that humanity has been reborn. You and your children now are the promise for the future.

The Child Assumes Responsibility

God put a rainbow in the sky as a sign of the permanency of His relationship with a humanity reborn. No matter what misgivings parents may have about their children, they reassure them that their love not only is unbroken but will flourish.[15] Humanity will be partners with God in remaking the world.

Adam was created from the earth. In this new world, Noah, you will be my partner to remake the earth. But this partnership carries new responsibilities.[16] I gave Adam only one prohibition: not to eat from the Tree of Knowledge of Good and Evil. Against this, he rebelled. In your hands, however, I now place all that dwells in the world. You are responsible for everything that stirs upon the earth. Unlike those who came before you, you may eat of the flesh of animals.

In your hands...
Based on
Genesis 9:2–3.

However, you must not eat flesh with its life-blood still in it. If you do, I will hold you accountable for all acts of violence. There will be a clear reckoning for all of human life: Whoever sheds blood, his blood shall be shed. This, then, is the covenant I establish with you and your descendants. If you fulfill My commandments, you shall be fertile and increase upon the earth.[17]

you must not eat...
Genesis 9:4–7.

Noah and his sons left the ark as the rainbow shone in the sky, proceeding with God's guarantee that there would be an everlasting relationship between heaven and earth, and knowing that they would be the beginning of a recreated and prosperous earth.

As Jacob thought of Noah and his family leaving the ark, he could not help but recall how he had felt the morning after his encounter with a mysterious presence by the shores of the Jabbok River. As he limped away after the struggle, which had lasted all night, he was warmed by the rays of the newly risen sun, bringing the dawn of a new day. He felt as if he had been reborn, that this was the beginning of his life, just as Noah must have felt:[18]

he had felt the morning...
Based on
Genesis 32:31–32.

Just look at the earth. You would think that there was nothing here before; there's not even a trace of vegetation left. It is impossible to think that everything our predecessors built has been destroyed. It is as if humanity has just been created. Worse, the Garden about which the ancients spoke also could not have survived the flood waters. Since God has spared us, it must be for the purpose of replenishing the world and replanting the Garden.

Noah was a tiller of the earth, just as Adam and Cain had been before him, but he did not simply care for what God had already planted. He took the initiative and planted a vineyard, thereby emulating his Divine parent. His first act after the Flood was to begin restoring God's garden.[19]

planted a vineyard...
Genesis 9:20.

The Child Lacks Inhibition and Propriety

Though Noah had matured enough to realize the power he possessed to change the world, he was still relatively young and needed some immediate gratification. After planting his vineyard and watching the grapes mature on the vine, he could not wait to taste the wine that he produced. Perhaps God should have reminded Noah about what had happened to Adam. Some ancients even say that the fruit Adam ate when violating God's commandment was also the fruit of the vine.[20] Or maybe Noah should have been mature enough by now to know that there would, indeed, be consequences to drinking too much wine. But lacking the self-control necessary to merely sample the wine, Noah drank to excess and fell into a drunken stupor.

Falling down on his bed of straw in his tent, Noah inadvertently uncovered himself, and he lay naked.[21] Then one of his three sons, Ham, entered the tent and saw his father naked for the first time. Like most children, he was overwhelmed by the sight. Yet, he did not turn and run, as we might expect. Rather, he drew close. Amazed by the size of his father's genitals, Ham touched them as if he wanted to see whether they were real. His curiosity and instincts had

uncovered himself...
Genesis 9:21–22.

gotten the best of him, and he violated his father. Rushing outside, he found his two brothers, Shem and Yapheth, and told them what he had done. Shem and Yapheth were embarrassed, both by what their brother had done and by their father's drunkenness and nudity. They did not want to see their father naked, nor acknowledge that he could lose control, as he had with his drinking. It is difficult for children to realize that a parent is not perfect, just as it is difficult for them to witness a parent's lack of propriety, whenever it may occur. So Shem and Yapfeth entered the tent and covered their father, all the while averting their eyes.

covered their father...
Genesis 9:23.

Such moments can erode a parent's self-esteem as well as a child's respect for the parent. They are also very embarrassing for the parent. Through the child's response to the parent's predicament, the parent also recognizes the essential nature of the child. If the child ridicules the parent, it speaks volumes about the type of person the child is. And so, when Noah woke up, he learned what Ham had done. He now knew the true nature of his own son. This was similar to what God had learned about the nature of humans from what Adam and Eve had done in the Garden.

God had learned...
An allusion to Genesis 8:21.

Jacob understood what Noah had gone through to come to know his children. He himself had twelve sons, all with very definite and very different personalities. He had come to know them through the many ways in which they related to him and to each other. He knew them so well that he could predict what would become of them in the future. And so, on his deathbed, he blessed them, each according to his past actions.

cursed him...
Genesis 9:25–26.

But Noah didn't bless Ham. He cursed him and predicted the future of his children:[22] "Cursed be Canaan, the son of Ham. He shall be the lowest of the slaves to his brothers.... Blessed be the Lord, the God of Shem; let Canaan be a slave to them. May God enlarge Yapheth, and let him dwell in the tents of Shem. And let Canaan be a slave to them." For all that it seemed to have achieved, humanity was still very young and very immature and had not developed a sense of propriety and self-control.

Canaan...
Genesis 9:25–27.
Ham was under-
stood to be the prog-
enitor of the
Canaanites.

The Child as a Developing Moral Agent

When Noah awoke from his drunken state, he was fully aware of the sin that his son Ham had committed. Noah knew what was right and what was wrong. This was evident when he condemned Ham. But Adam had hid when God confronted him, and he had taken no responsibility for eating from the fruit of the Tree. And Cain had denied any responsibility for his brother, Abel. Unlike his ancestors, Noah did not have the benefit of prior warning or prohibition, yet he and his sons were accountable for their actions.[23]

Noah knew...
Genesis 9:24.

But there is more. While it was God who punished Adam and Cain, it was Noah who uttered the curse upon Ham and his progeny. Not only did Ham bring the consequences upon himself, but Noah was the moral agent in this case—not God. By now, Noah had gained a sense of moral responsibility and showed a willingness to act upon it. This is typical of the moral development of most children. Told that "whoever sheds the blood of another human being, his blood shall be shed by human beings," Noah was ready to carry out justice on God's behalf. By this action, it was apparent that Noah and his sons now governed the world that they would populate and shape.[24]

whoever sheds...
Genesis 9:6.

For the first time, God, who was Noah's parent, felt that the child could clearly distinguish between what is right and wrong and could be trusted to act on his or her own. Noah established a hierarchy among his children based upon their actions. Shem and Yapheth, in contrast to Ham, deserved to be rewarded. The meritocracy created by Noah, however rudimentary it may have been, illustrated his developing maturity. As a result, God felt closer to Noah than He had to any of his predecessors, relating to **speaking to him...** him and speaking to him in ways that Adam and Eve and See Bereshit Rabbah Cain had never experienced. As God's partner, Noah would 34:5 in this regard. shape a new world, and God would savor the consolation and the hope that Noah and his family represented.

CHAPTER FOUR

THE PEOPLE OF SHINAR
(and the Tower of Babel)

Pre-Adolescence

Erik Erikson: Stage Four
Industry vs. Inferiority

- The individual begins to be productive as a worker and a provider. Ego-strength is measured by competence in workmanship and the ability to complete a task.
- There is an expanding curiosity about all things and a willingness to experiment with new skills and handle new implements.
- The danger is feeling inadequate or inferior to others or being unable to use skills or tools or to be productive. Also, if what individuals produce is their only measure of self-worth, then they will become slaves to their vocation.
- This is the time for youngsters to broaden their circle outside their own families, to collaborate with peers and gain validation from them. Achievement begins to be viewed in terms of the group's success. The adolescent learns the perspective of others and the need to respect individuality and to trust others.
- This may also be a time of struggling to control one's impulses and to harness one's exuberant imagination. Taking charge of one's life can lead to a new sense of freedom, power, and independence.

As Jacob thought about what had transpired after the Flood he recalled how humanity had tried to build a tower that would reach the heavens:

climbing a
ladder...
Based on
Genesis 28:12–18.

I understood their need to feel close to God, even to see themselves as God-like. For I had once dreamed of climbing a ladder on which I could ascend to heaven. But, as it happened, I awoke to learn that reaching heaven is possible only in a dream. And though we are merely human, we can gain a sense of God's presence right here on earth.

Moving Beyond the Family: Humanity Building Together

Exiting from the ark, Noah's sons went their separate ways. Although they spread far and wide during the generations following the Flood, they were bound by the same language and history. The small family that had survived the Flood in a womb-like ark had blossomed into the entire family of nations.

the same
language...
Genesis 11:1.

family of nations...
Genesis 10:32.

valley in
the land...
Genesis 11:2.

In time, the peoples of the earth moved westward. Many settled in a beautiful, fertile valley in the land of Shinar.[1] Even though they were divided into many distinct families, the people of Shinar understood that their future depended upon their ability to work together toward a common goal:[2]

let us work...
Based on
Genesis 11:3–4.

Come, friends, let us work as one family.[3] Our only hope for survival is to band together and pool our resources and talents. If we fail to do so, we will never survive. Doing more than simply farming the land will require that we plan and build as if we were one. If we are to settle here in the Valley of Shinar and create a life for ourselves, we need to erect something of permanence, just as our ancestors spoke of Cain, who built a city and named it after his son, Enoch. He understood that his future, symbolized by his son, could be ensured only if he erected a place in which he and his progeny would dwell. Let

built a city...
Genesis 4:17.

us begin by building homes for all our families, a place where we can live and flourish.

Human beings began to realize that they have the ability to work cooperatively with others and, by doing so, enhance their own future. Through their work, they could move beyond the world of their parents and gain greater autonomy and a greater sense of themselves. By working with their peers, they affirmed who they were in ways that had not been possible in their nuclear families. They were eager to work in partnership with others and to use their common language to create together.

Developing Skills: Building a Tower

The people who settled in the Valley of Shinar immediately began building a city. But to do so they had to create materials that would serve their efforts. They shaped the soil into bricks, then baked them until they were stone-hard. These were produced in large numbers and with much less effort than that required by breaking stones into the shapes needed for construction.

bricks, then baked... Based on Genesis 11:3.

They noticed that engulfing clumps of soil in hot flames made them very hard. After several unsuccessful attempts at hardening shaped blocks of soil, they realized that the flame had to be contained for the soil to bake. Once they built stone boxes to hold the blocks, they could produce as many bricks as they needed. The larger the kilns, as these boxes were called, the more bricks they made.

But how would they ensure that the structures they built would remain standing? What would hold the bricks together? This problem was solved when they discovered that burning certain kinds of rock produced a black, liquid substance, which, upon cooling, was so solid that it could hardly be chipped. This bitumen led the people who dwelled in the Valley of Shinar to start contemplating heaping brick upon brick to erect large structures:[4]

> Now that we know how to make large quantities of bricks and have figured out how to shape them into structures that will stand, let's build a city in which we can live for the rest of our lives. If we don't, we will always be at the mercy of nature. The great winds from the desert can come at any time during the hot season and destroy everything made of wood and fabric. If we don't construct permanent buildings, we'll forever be destined to move from place to place in search of safe domiciles. And what will become of us? We will be scattered over the face of the earth.
>
> We won't be building only a secure place that is our own, but also a place that shows our greatness. We'll build a tower that will reach to the very vaults of heaven. Since we are created in the image of the Creator, we have the power to connect heaven and earth. Our tower will be visible for miles and miles, and every time we see it, we will be reminded of our divine origins.

scattered over...
Genesis 11:4.

The people of Shinar were like maturing children who begin to develop their egos by recognizing what they are capable of producing or building. Childhood games that involve building blocks are eventually replaced by erecting actual skyscrapers that can be noticed by everyone. The taller the building, the more skillful, industrious, and powerful the builder is thought to be. The tower erected in the Valley of Shinar demonstrated just how far people had journeyed from the garden of their infancy, a garden in which they were totally dependent upon God.

Making a Name for Themselves: Illusory Power

The people of Shinar began to build their city and the tower that would reach to heaven. They didn't want to only create a place in which they and their descendants could

live securely; they also wanted to make a name for them- **make a name...**
Genesis 11:4.
selves. They needed to demonstrate their power, skill, and
autonomy. They wanted to show that they could do anything on which they set their minds, anything they could
imagine. They wanted to prove that they didn't need God
for anything.[5]

> Now that we know how to make bricks and bitumen, we can
> erect the strongest and tallest structures that will withstand
> all the forces of nature. Even if God were to bring a flood
> again, as in the days of Noah, our city would remain standing;
> our lives would remain intact. We will never again be scat- **scattered over...**
> tered over the face of the earth. Genesis 11:4.
>
> We have the ability not only to ensure our survival but to
> recreate the very Garden from which our ancestors were
> banished. Nothing is out of our reach. By using our knowl-
> edge and skills, we can emulate God and create a new world.
> Through work, our lives will find meaning.

God could not understand what had become of humanity. Only a few generations had passed since the Flood had
destroyed the world, and Noah and his family had been
given an opportunity to start the chain of life all over again.
Seeing the new tower and realizing that building it had to
do with their own self-aggrandizement, God again began to
bemoan that he had ever created humans:

> This is how they have begun to act! Like their ancestor **have begun**
> Adam, they rebel against Me. They profane My name.[6] After **to act...**
> Genesis 11:6.
> preparing the Garden of Eden for Adam and providing
> humanity with everything necessary for it to flourish, Adam
> did not appreciate what I had done. It was as if I didn't exist.
> Adam thought he could do anything, including disobeying
> My commandment. How ungrateful: to ignore Me after all
> that I had done! The people of Shinar are no better.[7] They,
> too, devise lofty plans without thinking of Me. They feel that
> nothing is out of their reach. Well, they must learn that their **nothing is out...**
> Genesis 11:6.

cunning will not be rewarded. The evil that the Tower represents must be undone. They must learn that they are not God and that the power they think they possess is illusory.[8]

The people of Shinar, who built their tower as if it demonstrated their God-like powers, were similar to most young people who have yet to learn that they are not omnipotent. They believed they had the power to change the world on their own, and they could not see their own limitations. They did not realize that the true power in the universe resides elsewhere and that it is certainly not found in the technology they had discovered. Every generation must come to its own understanding that the heavens are beyond the reach of humans. Every generation must develop its own humility and struggle with its own hubris.

The Path to Isolation and Loneliness

Just when young people think that everything is in their control, that they have the power to determine their future and the imagination and ingenuity needed to overcome every obstacle, something happens to bring them back to earth and ruin all their grandiose plans.

As Jacob thought of the people of Shinar dreaming of building a tower that would reach to the heavens, he also thought of Joseph, who was now on his way to his tent with his two sons. Joseph, too, had once had grandiose dreams. His dream was that the sun, the moon, and the stars were all bowing down to him. Like the builders of the Tower, Joseph felt that he had a power that made him special and unique among his brothers. But his dreams ended in a pit near Shechem, where his brothers had thrown him and then sold him to a passing caravan. They wanted to get rid of their younger brother, their father's favorite son, who constantly lauded himself over them. All this was the result of Joseph's overbearing ego. Just as in the story of the Tower, it was God who determined Joseph's fate. Jacob could imagine God talking to Himself:

> If they think that they are capable of building towers that will reach to the heavens, then they must learn their place in this world. No amount of cooperation and hard work, no matter how skillfully done, can guarantee success on earth if the goal of the people is to be like Me. Ultimately, they won't even be able to work together. Each one will come to feel as though he or she is more important or more skilled than everyone else, and their apparent unity of purpose will disappear. The only real unity in the world is found in Me. Human beings can begin to experience this unity only when they sacrifice their own drive for personal recognition and power.[9] I will go down and confound their speech so they will not understand one another. Then they will begin arguing, and soon won't even be able to work together.

I will go down...
Based on
Genesis 11:7.

The harmony that had existed when the people began building the city and the Tower quickly dissipated. Each group of artisans—the brick makers, the brick carriers, the erectors of the scaffolding, the architects, the masons—was concerned only about its specific task. Each group felt that it was indispensable—that without it, the Tower would never be built. As a result, the groups began to bicker with each other. Anything that one worker said was utterly misunderstood by a co-worker. Each felt that the other was harsh and hurtful. In a matter of days, the site upon which the Tower was being built was totally vacant. The workers had retreated into small groups and refused to have anything to do with each other.

was totally vacant...
Genesis 11:8.

Leaving the Valley: Giving Up the Ego

Unlike the generation of the Flood, the builders of the Tower were not destroyed. By working together, they showed that they had matured to some degree beyond the people who had perished in the Flood, even if they had built the Tower for their own egotistical ends. So, God decided not to destroy them but to scatter them over the face of the earth:[10]

Although they worked together building the Tower, they really don't understand or care for one another. Maybe they shared the same language, but that is all they shared. Each human being cares only for himself or herself. They were convinced that being able to erect monuments to themselves would give their lives meaning and that who they were would be determined by the height of their Tower.

But their Tower is really an illusion, as is their power. It simply led to a loss of their true selves and, in the process, to a separation from each other. What they said to each other to demonstrate their prowess only drove them apart. If they truly had spoken to one another's hearts, if they had listened to one another and felt for one another, then their efforts would have succeeded. They would have been able to build one community out of their many families. Words, if they are used for selfish purposes, can separate people from one another.

At times, words can simply be the "babble" of self-aggrandizement. But they can also bring people together. That is what the people of the Valley must learn. By accepting the differences in the way each person speaks, perhaps while even using the same language, they will come to know each other. True communication depends upon listening with the heart. Words can lead to separation, but they can also unite people and make them one.[11]

Soon, different groups began to leave the Valley of Shinar, scattering in all directions. What had once promised to be the Eden recreated was now a desolate valley that echoed with empty words, the vestiges of a dream that had evaporated and died. Just as their ancient descendants had had to leave the Garden of Eden so they could grow and mature outside of the nurturing womb, so, too, the people of Shinar had to move beyond the valley of their ego-inflated vision so they could arrive at their real place in the world. That place—the garden of their maturity—would one day be built upon the unity of the human family shaped in the image of the one God of the universe.

scattering...
Based on
Genesis 11:8–9

CHAPTER FIVE

ABRAHAM

Adolescence

Erik Erikson: Stage Five
Identity vs. Role Confusion

- Disengagement from one's parental home and establishment of one's own identity. The adolescent gives up previous objects of love, primarily the family, and invests energy in causes and in other people. This often involves the rejection or modification of the parents' or of the original group's religious ideas or values.
- Egocentrism changes to concern for others. The ability to fulfill personal potential while responding to peers becomes more prominent, along with the development of social contracts and universal principles. Peer group membership bolsters self-esteem.
- Fidelity is pledged to the group and to its sense of manifest destiny. Defending the group is crucial. Clannish behavior leads to excluding those who are different.
- Rituals change a juvenile sense of omnipotence into group identity and confirm group membership.
- Attempts are made to clearly define one's identity and to attain an inner coherence, a durable set of values, and a concrete worldview. The adolescent begins thinking in ideological terms, abstractions, and ideals.

As Jacob's mind wandered back to the attempt of the people of the Valley of Shinar to feel God-like he understood that humanity's journey to maturity was slow and arduous. By its very nature, it would proceed in stages, and by necessity, this would involve surrendering the self to the Divine. Human beings would have to learn that true stature would come not by building a tower to reach the heavens but by surrendering their egos to make room for God in their lives. Only through a covenant with God would men and women come to wholeness. Jacob also knew that the beginning of the journey that led to the covenant between his ancestors and God had begun with his grandfather, Abraham.[1]

Following in Our Parent's Footsteps

From all that Jacob had heard about his grandfather, he had always sensed that they were very much alike. In contrast to Jacob's father, Isaac, Abraham and Jacob had both had to set out on their own to discover their true place in life. Ironically, both of these life journeys were closely linked to their fathers' journeys. Jacob had finally understood how Abraham's path in life was in part charted by his father, Terah, and he was sure that this is how Abraham would have described his journey:

grew up in Southern Mesopotamia... All this is based on Genesis 11:27–31.

I grew up in Southern Mesopotamia, in a place called Ur. I had two younger brothers, Nahor and Haran. All of us married, and I took Sarah, who then was called Sarai, to be my wife. We had every intention of living out our lives in Ur, which was a rather large city near the mouth of the Euphrates River. Tragically, however, my brother Haran died suddenly, and my family never recovered.

Soon, my father decided that the family would leave Ur and start a new life elsewhere. In a few weeks, all of us except Nahor and his wife packed our belongings and followed our father as he set out on the arduous journey up the Fertile Crescent and down the King's Highway along the Big Sea. We wanted to create a new life in faraway Canaan. After what seemed to be an endless trek, we reached the city of Haran in Northern Mesopotamia. This would be our resting place for a few weeks before we continued south toward Canaan. But as it turns out, we never left for Canaan. My father never actually decided that we would settle permanently in Haran, yet this became his permanent resting place.

became his permanent resting place... Genesis 11:32.

I don't know why my father didn't continue his journey to Canaan. After all, that was his dream from the very beginning. Perhaps he was just too tired; getting to Haran took everything out of him. Or maybe he was pleased with what he found in Haran. Whatever the reason, I knew that one day I would complete the journey.

Like most young people, Abraham was shaped in part by his father and by growing up in his parents' home. He not only joined his father on the journey from Ur, but shared the dream of some day starting a new life in Canaan. And though there were moments when he thought of taking his wife and their servants and leaving Haran while Terah was alive, he could not abandon his elderly father. He thought to himself, "Shall I leave and bring dishonor upon myself and upon the Divine name, as people will say: 'He left his father in his old age and departed'?" Had it not been for God's call to Abraham, he probably would have died in Haran just as his father had:

He thought to himself... Bereshit Rabbah 39:7.

Abraham, it is time for you to start out on your own life journey. Just as your father left Ur to follow his dream of a new life, you, too, must go forth from your land and from your father's house to the land that I will show you. Go! I free you from responsibility for your father, who will live well without you and will die at a ripe old age.[2]

go forth... Genesis 12:1.

Realizing his father's mortality, Abraham was moved perhaps to fulfill his father's dream of journeying to Canaan. The voice he heard propelled him into the future. He had already shared part of his father's journey, and now he knew that he must complete it: He was inheriting Terah's legacy even while extending it and even surpassing it.[3]

Leaving Behind the Past: Journeying into the Unknown

Jacob surely understood what it meant for the young Abraham to be called to leave his homeland and his father's house. He remembered vividly the day he had to flee from his parents' home and set out on his own journey to Haran. In effect, he had retraced Abraham's steps. By doing this, he had had experienced how wrenching yourself from what is meaningful to you can lead to greater self-knowledge and also to realizing the potential for creating your own family.

> flee from his parents'...
> Genesis 27:43ff.

Until Abraham could distance himself from what had defined him as an adolescent—the culture, mythology, and mores of the society in which he was raised, and his family's customs and stories—he could not begin to search for his real self. He had begun to recognize that he existed separately from the surroundings of his youth. In turn, this realization propelled him toward his ultimate destiny.[4] The moment he was called from his parents' home, he began to create a new generation, one that was based, in part, upon what his ancestors had bequeathed him.[5]

> It is time for me to leave Haran—to set out on my own and build a life for myself, for my wife, and our future family. I know that this is what God wants me to do. But where shall we go? In what direction shall we travel? God has not revealed the destination. It almost seems that the Divine has not done this on purpose.

Perhaps that is the point of it all: We human beings live in an imperfect world in which the path we must take is not very clear. God wants us to find the way for ourselves. If God had wanted me to complete my father's journey to Canaan, it would have been easy for God to have commanded me, saying, "Go forth from your native land, from your father's house to the land of Canaan." Yet, what I felt God saying to me was "Go forth…to the land that I will show you."

to the land…
Genesis 12:1.

Although I trust God and myself to find the way, I want to be sure that this is the path my life should take. Most of the time, I feel certain that I should continue in my father's footsteps and head southward. Yet, how can I be certain? The only choice I have is to begin the journey, though feeling unsure, in the hope that my destiny will become more evident to me along the way.[6]

The Journey to Canaan: Journeying Inward by Stages

Abraham had difficulty knowing the direction that his life journey should take precisely because he was on a journey of self-discovery. This is the force of God's command to him:

The Lord said to Abraham, "*Lech lecha* [Go to yourself]." Abraham, you must journey inward and come to know yourself and what is important to you.[7] You must find out who you are. In order to do so, you must leave your land, your father's house, and set out on your own journey. You have to distinguish yourself from your home and family in order to recognize yourself as a separate person. If you set forth on this path, I will make you into a great nation and I will bless you. It will be as if I have created you anew; it will be nothing short of a transformation of self. Blessing will come to you when you gain a firm sense of who you are and what the essence of your life is all about.

leave your land…
Based on
Genesis 12:1.

created you anew…
Based on the interpretation of Genesis 12:2 in Midrash Tanhuma ha-Nidpas, Lech Lecha 4.

The journey of self-realization is never easy. It proceeds in stages and does not unfold overnight. It takes a long time and demands patience.

Jacob knew about journeying inward and the difficulty of doing this. He remembered all that he had gone through in the twenty years he had lived in Laban's house. These experiences had taught him who he was and what God expected of him. He recalled confronting and later reconciling with his brother, Esau, and the dream-like struggle with an angel on the bank of the Jabbok. Those twenty years had involved innumerable opportunities for growth; they had prepared him for his role as patriarch. The same occurred with Abraham's journey from Haran to Canaan. This was Abraham's journey to maturity, one that would not be easy. God had so much as told him this:

> Abraham, you stand at a major crossroad in your life. Haran is a turning point for you.[8] You have already experienced what it was like to leave your native country. You learned about the hardship of leaving behind family and friends, and starting out on your own. But you were still quite young then, and the full impact of the change might not have been so clear to you. So you now must uproot yourself again, and leave behind the land you have come to know as your own and all that it has meant to you.[9] More painfully, however, you must bid farewell to your father and your family, all of whom you probably will never see again.

The physical hardship of traveling to Canaan and the emotional difficulty of uprooting himself from his culture and society and family were very difficult, as they are for all young people—and their parents.[10] Leaving home challenges everything that we have come to know: our physical surroundings, lifestyle, values, and long standing familial or communal beliefs. Yet, this is an essential step on the path to maturity, a path that has many stages and many challenges, some of which are not even evident at the time.[11]

Abraham passed through the land of Canaan, came to the city of Shechem, and built an altar to God at Alon Moreh. After proceeding on to Beth El, he built another altar there. Then he, Sarah, Lot, and their clan headed south. They finally came to the Negev but decided to continue on to Egypt because of the severe drought.[12]

the city of Shechem... Genesis 12:6–9.

Abraham's journey occurred in increments, just as his search for himself and the meaning of his life involved a protracted struggle within himself and with those whom he loved.

Struggling with the Other to Protect Our Self

Although Abraham's goal was to settle in Canaan, the land that God had destined for him, he could not recognize the place that God had intended because of the famine in Canaan.[13] But by continuing on down to Egypt, Abraham showed that he had not matured spiritually enough to put down roots in the land promised to him by God. He lacked sufficient faith in the power of the Divine.[14]

the land... Genesis 12:1, 5.

continuing on down... Genesis 12:10.

His lack of maturity was also evident in his words and actions once he arrived in Egypt. As he approached the border of Egypt he said to his Sarai, his wife:

Behold, I know that you are beautiful.... When the Egyptians see you, they will desire you and they will kill me. If you love me and care about me and our future together, please say that you are my sister so that it may go well for me because of you. We have been through so much since we left Aram Naharaim years ago. We have shared a life journey to the land to which God has led us. And now, as we enter this foreign place whose inhabitants are swarthy and mean, our lives are in your hands.[15]

Behold, I know... Based on Genesis 12:11–13.

About to confront potential adversaries, Abraham was more concerned about his safety than about Sarah and her feelings. He seemed willing to sacrifice his relationship with her to ensure his survival. For the moment, Sarah was unimportant: a nonentity, an unnamed object who could be taken into the Pharoah's harem and sacrificed for Abraham's sake.

a nonentity...
Based on
Genesis 12:15.

His willingness to sacrifice Sarah demonstrated his lack of maturity. Later, he began to understand that there was a kinship between himself and his nephew, Lot. He showed this by his referring to Lot as his brother. This would set them apart from the other inhabitants of Canaan. Yet, Abraham also saw Lot as a rival who threatened his turf. Again, Abraham was only concerned about himself:

his brother...
Genesis 13:8.

Lot's flocks...
Abraham's words are based on Genesis 13:5–9.

Lot's flocks and herds have grown in size, and there is simply not enough land to support both of us. Our possessions are so many that we cannot stay together any longer.[16] We must separate if we are to survive. Let's divide up the land so there will be no strife between us.... But how can I send Lot away? After all, he is my dead brother's son, and I pledged to protect and care for him. He has been like my brother all these years, taking Haran's place in my life ever since he died. Yet, I have no choice. It is a matter of survival. I'm sure that Lot will understand when I put it to him in that way.

Jacob could empathize with Abraham's struggle with Lot because of his own difficult relationship with Esau. He, too, had fought with "his brother" over the right to the land and its inherent blessings. He also understood the great pain that Abraham experienced because of the tension between his wife, Sarah, and her handmaid, Hagar. Jacob bore many emotional scars from the years of turmoil in Laban's house involving Rachel and Leah and their handmaids. Just as his conflict with Esau was mirrored in the relationship between Jacob's two wives, Abraham's adolescent struggle with Lot was reflected in the strife that developed some time later between Sarah and Hagar.

Concerned that she had been unable to become pregnant and provide an heir for her husband, Sarah voluntarily gave Hagar to Abraham to elevate herself in his eyes. Sarah was initially only concerned about her role as provider for her husband. But after giving Hagar to Abraham, she despaired even more over her status and what people would think of her:

> I can't believe it. Just when I thought that giving Hagar to Abraham as his concubine would make him appreciate me even more, the trouble really began. When Hagar saw that she had conceived, she bragged and taunted me incessantly. When women from the village would come to inquire about me, Hagar would say to them, "My mistress is not inwardly what she appears to be outwardly. For had she been righteous, so many years would not have passed without her conceiving. Yet, I conceived in one night." But it really is not Hagar's fault. She doesn't know any better. She's a mere Egyptian handmaid. But where is my husband when I need him?[17] "Abraham, the wrong done to me is your fault. When I speak to Hagar in front of you and she ridicules me, you do not respond to her. You are my husband. Why do you remain silent?"[18]

Like most young people, Sarah projected onto others her own feelings of inadequacy, and Abraham bore the brunt of her negative self-perception. Yet, Abraham did have the opportunity to alleviate some of Sarah's pain and the tension between her and Hagar. But he was not mature enough to intervene effectively. By remaining passive, he abdicated his responsibility to both women. He meekly told Sarah to deal with Hagar as she saw fit—and that let her take out all of her frustrations on Hagar.[19]

unable to become pregnant...
Based on Genesis 16:1–3.

When Hagar saw...
Genesis 16:4.

Abraham, the wrong...
Genesis 16:5.
When I speak...
Sefer ha-Yashar on Lech Lecha.

Sarah to deal...
Based on Genesis 16:6.

Both Abraham and Sarah had not yet matured to the point of being truly concerned for others, even those they love.

Seeing Ourselves As Part of a Group

Yet, from the very start of his journey to Canaan, Abraham was told that his identity would be defined by the nation to which he would give birth. God had made that very clear to him:

I will make...
Based on
Genesis 12:2–3.

Abraham, I will make of you a great nation, and through it your name shall also be made great. And all the families of the earth shall be blessed through your actions and those of your people. Those who bless you shall be blessed; but those who curse you and your people, they themselves shall be cursed.

So, as Jacob thought about the beginnings of his people and the promises that God had made to Abraham, which had been fulfilled in Jacob's lifetime, he realized that Abraham probably had not yet appreciated the importance of God's words. How should he, as a young person, understand that his identity largely depended on the group to which he belonged, a group with a unique destiny that set it apart from all other nations? But that was exactly what God had conveyed to Abraham the very first time that he experienced the Divine presence.

he took along...
Based on the
rabbinic
interpretation of
Genesis 12:5. See,
for example,
Shir ha-Shirim
Rabbah 1:3:3.

Abraham would quickly learn, however, that those who were willing to become part of his people deserved his fidelity and support. As he started for Canaan he took along everyone who had joined him in his belief in the one God and in the future promise of his people. It was that promise of future greatness which God emphasized to Abraham when he returned to Canaan from Egypt, when the Lord said that all of Canaan would belong to him and to his offspring. Possession of the land of Canaan would set Abraham and his family apart from those who already dwelt in the land: the Perizzites and the Canaanites. There was a necessary loyalty among the members of their clan and an attachment to the land that would transcend all personal friction. Abraham was learning what *belonging* to a tribe meant:

all of Canaan...
Genesis 12:7.

those who already...
Genesis 13:7.

> Lot, I see that our herdsmen constantly argue over their grazing land. Our flocks and herds are so large that they seem to think that there is not sufficient land to accommodate both of our families. Why should there be any strife between us, especially when we realize that we face a common enemy who lives in this land? We kinsmen share a common destiny—God has promised this land to us and to our children. Let us separate and choose different places to dwell. If you go north, I will go south; if you go south, I will travel north.

I see that our herdsmen...
Based on Genesis 13:7–10.

Lot chose the plain of Jordan in which to settle, and traveled eastward. God told Abraham to gaze upon the land in its entirety, promising to give it all to him and to his descendants forever. God commanded him to walk the length and breadth of Canaan. Doing this would define its limits, and Abraham could take possession of it in perpetuity. In a sense, the land that would belong to him would be defined by what he saw and what he did.[20]

gaze upon the land...
Genesis 13:14–17.

Walking the land was almost a ritual that confirmed his right to the territory which God had promised. In a most primitive manner, he had to walk the land before he could settle on it. Once he took possession of the land for himself and his people, he pitched his tent in Hebron.

pitched his tent...
Genesis 13:18.

But how could Abraham, like the maturing person he was, be sure that the land would indeed belong to him and to his people? How could he be sure that the relationship

he had no children...
Genesis 15:2–3.

will not be your heir...
Genesis 15:4–10.

the sun set...
Genesis 15:17–18.

God promise...
Based on Genesis 15:12–16.

become fertile...
Based on Genesis 17:2–8.

between him and the God he had come to know would be sealed forever, given the fact that he had no children? Perhaps his servant Eliezer would become his heir. God, however, assured Abraham of his future:

Eliezer will not be your heir; your very own issue shall guarantee your future. Look toward the heavens and count the stars. So shall your offspring be numerous. I am the Lord who brought you from Ur so I could give you this land as a permanent possession. Let us enter into a covenant which will affirm the relationship between Me and you and your descendants forever. Bring Me a three-year-old heifer, a three-year-old she-goat, a three-year-old ram, a turtledove, and a young bird. Cut them in two, placing each half opposite the other.

When the sun set and it was very dark, there miraculously appeared a smoking oven and a flaming torch. These symbolized the Divine presence. On that day, God made a brit, a covenant with Abraham, and guaranteed to Abraham's offspring the land of Canaan, from the river of Egypt to the river Euphrates.[21]

This unconditional commitment from God would provide the basis for his people's belief that they would survive. And indeed, in the midst of the ritual, a deep sleep overcame Abraham, and he heard God promise him that even though his children would be forced to leave the land and would be oppressed for four hundred years, they would surely return to the land of Canaan and live in peace.[22]

The promise of the future was now secure: God had established an everlasting covenant with Abraham, who would become fertile and be the father of an entire nation. The land of Canaan would be theirs forever, and the Divine would be their God forever.

Once again, to reiterate the covenant between the Divine and Abraham's family, a sacred ritual would be necessary. But this time it would not be God's presence passing through the pieces of sacrifice, but rather Abraham himself, marking their unique family identity that bound one generation to the next.[23] As God said:

> Such shall be the covenant between Me and you and all your offspring to follow: Every male among you shall be circumcised. You shall circumcise the flesh of your foreskin, and that shall be a sign of the covenant between Me and you. Throughout the generations, every male among you shall be circumcised at the age of eight days. Anyone who does not circumcise the flesh of his foreskin has broken My covenant and will be cut off from this people.

Such shall be... Genesis 17:10–14.

The physical change involved in circumcision represented for Abraham and his family the essential transformation that they had experienced: becoming a people devoted to living in covenantal relationship with the one God to whom they were tied forever. This change in their very natures was underscored by God's altering their names. Abraham and Sarah shed their original names as a sign of their future promise of greatness: They would be the progenitors of a multitude of nations, and their son, to whom Sarah would give birth, would carry on their line.

progenitors... Based on Genesis 17:5–6, 15–16.

Abraham, like most maturing individuals, had found meaning and identity in the group to which he had devoted his life. And as the progenitor of the group, he set his focus on conveying a set of enduring values and a coherent worldview to others.

Moving Beyond the Group: Responding to the Other

Abraham remained devoted to his covenanted community, and especially to his family. When powerful kings from the East conquered land in and around Canaan, and seized the wealth of Sodom and Gomorrah and captured many

powerful kings... Based on Genesis 14:1–11.

people, Abraham did not hesitate to act. Hearing that Lot
had been captured, he pursued the enemy as far as Hovah,
a city north of Damascus, defeated them, and brought back
Lot and his possessions, as well as all the captured inhabitants of Sodom and Gomorrah and all of their possessions.[24] When his relatives were in trouble, Abraham
showed that he understood the responsibilities attendant
on being a member of a clan. Fidelity to the group and
defending it are crucial for all young persons as they
mature. Yet, even under these circumstances, Abraham
recognized his obligation to others as well. When he
returned from battle and Melchizedek, the king of Salem,
blessed him and his God, Abraham unhesitatingly gave
Melchizedek a tenth of all the spoils that he had won. He
showed his new maturity not only by helping to defend his
kinsmen and neighbors but also by his new sense of ethics.
Thankful for what Abraham had done, the king of Sodom
told him to keep the possessions that he had won back. But
Abraham refused:

will not keep...
Based on
Genesis 14:19–24.

> I cannot possibly think of taking anything that does not right-
> fully belong to me and my people. I will not keep so much as
> a thread or a sandal strap that belongs to you. I simply did
> what was right and honorable. I did what God expected of
> me. To take anything of yours now would be a blasphemy. As
> for those who joined me—my allies, Aner and Eshkol—let
> them take their rightful shares.[25]

A maturing Abraham was able to reach beyond himself
and his group loyalties and to respond to others, even those
he did not know personally. He would even sit in the shade
of the entrance to his tent day after day, no matter how hot
it was, to watch for passing wayfarers in the desert. Then
he would invite them into his tent, pleased to provide them
with food, drink, and a place to refresh themselves:

sit in the shade...
Based on several
classic *midrashim*,
including Midrash
ha-Gadol to
Genesis 18:1.

Please, my lords, don't rush past. Allow me the pleasure of serving you. I will bring some water. Bathe your feet; wash and refresh yourselves. Good, good. Sit down, rest, and I will return momentarily…. Sarah, Sarah, come quickly. Take three measures of choice flour, and knead some fine cakes. While they rest, I will run to the herds and fetch a fine calf, and have it prepared for dinner. Let's treat these wayfarers as honored guests in our house.

Please, my lords…
Based on
Genesis 18:3–8.

Abraham developed a genuine concern for others, even if they weren't part of his family group. When informed by God that Sodom and Gomorrah would be destroyed because the people living there were sinful, Abraham did not hesitate to intercede on behalf of the innocent, even though they were strangers to him. He called God to task, reminding God of what is ethically correct: "How can the Judge of all the Earth not act justly?" He put himself on the line for the possible handful of righteous strangers who might deserve to be saved, even though he had no personal relationship with them.

God to task…
See Genesis
18:23–32.

Although Abraham was coming to understand his responsibility to other people, he had not yet fully matured. At certain moments, he was still concerned only about himself and his survival. Jacob could understand how, at times, Abraham reverted to his immature ways. He, himself, remembered how after struggling to become Israel, which signified his maturation, he still acted like the immature, manipulative "Jacob" he had once been.

to become Israel…
Genesis 32:29.

Such was the case with Abraham, who also reverted to his immature ways. This occurred, for instance, when he and his family traveled in the territory of Gerar and he was frightened that he would be killed because the men would lust after Sarah. So, as had happened many years before in Egypt, he claimed that Sarah was his sister. As a result,

"Jacob"…
See Genesis 35:10,
in which God has to
remind him of his
new name, Israel, as
if he had forgotten.
in the territory…
See the narrative in
Genesis 20.

Avimelech, the king of Gerar, took Sarah into his house. Abraham initially saw the people of Gerar as adversaries who could not be trusted, and he set himself apart from them. He was even willing to impose himself on Sarah, saying, "Let this be the kindness that you will do for me: Whatever place we come to, say there of me: 'He is my brother.'" Sarah again bore the pain of Abraham's insecurity, and Abraham reverted to an adolescent's concern only about himself.

Let this be...
Genesis 20:13.

Yet, even at this juncture, as he was struggling with his sense of self in relation to other human beings, including those whom he loved, we see signs of growth. When Avimelech's household was punished with infertility because he had taken Sarah into his harem, Abraham himself prayed on behalf of Avimelech and his wives:

Abraham himself prayed...
Genesis 20:17–18.
O Lord of the world...
Based on Bereshit Rabbah 52:13.

O Lord of the world, You have created us that we may increase and propagate. Grant that Avimelech and his household may themselves multiply and increase. Avimelech has shown me much kindness. He has restored my wife, Sarah, to me, and offered us any plot of land on which to settle in his kingdom. Please restore him and his wives and concubines to full health.

God granted Abraham's pleas. It is said that this was the first time in history when God fulfilled the prayer of one human being for the benefit of another. As a result, Avimelech enjoyed many progeny.

How fitting that as Abraham reached a level of maturity, as he began empathizing with others, he and Sarah became fertile.[26] God took note of Sarah, and she conceived and bore a son to Abraham in his old age.[27]

The change in Abraham was most evident in the way he related to Avimelech. Some time after the incident with Sarah, Abraham responded to Avimelech's urging that they make a pact of friendship and loyalty. Abraham swore that he would not deal falsely with Avimelech or his kin, or with the land in which he was sojourning. Abraham had matured to the point where he could live in peace in the land of the Philistines. When human beings can live together in harmony, then the place in which they dwell is surely a place of holiness.

place of holiness...
See Genesis
21:32–33, in which
Abraham and
Avimelech sign a
pact at Be'er Sheva
and plant a tamarisk
tree, invoking God's
presence.

Struggling with Our Egos:
Coming to Grips with Our Dark Sides

The journey toward maturity involves struggling with the darkest sides of ourselves. Jacob understood this very well, since he had wrestled for much of his life with his shadow. From the stealing of his brother's birthright to his nocturnal struggle on the shore of the Jabbok River, Jacob had constantly had to overcome much to feel whole. But his greatest personal pain came when he had to deal with his children. Abraham had had a similar struggle, a struggle with the shadows of his own persona as he related to his own sons, Ishmael and Isaac.[28]

With the birth of Isaac, not only did God fulfill His promise to Abraham and Sarah, but Abraham was given a guarantor for his future. His role as the father of a large, important nation would be carried out through Sarah's son. Though he may have loved Ishmael, his future depended solely upon Isaac.

His promise...
Made by the three
visitors in
Genesis 18:10.

Soon after Isaac was weaned, Sarah tested Abraham's sense of his true identity and his fidelity to the promise that Isaac would be his heir by demanding that he banish Ishmael and Hagar from their home. The future of Abraham's people depended upon his being able to clearly set his priorities, at least in Sarah's eyes. In his developing maturity, Abraham yielded to Sarah's request. But he did it

banish...
Genesis 21:10.

**God had
told him...**
Genesis 21:12.

not necessarily to please Sarah, but because God had told
him that through Isaac his future would be assured. God's
promise that Ishmael would survive and flourish impelled
Abraham to send Ishmael and Hagar into the harsh, barren
desert. More than all the other misfortunes that befell
Abraham in his life, this was the most painful:

most painful...
Pirkei d'Rabbi
Eliezer, Chapter 30,
based on
Genesis 21:11.

> But he's my son![29] How can I possibly do as Sarah has said. I
> know that the future of our people is bound up with Isaac,
> but I simply cannot cast off my son. It would be as if I cut off
> one of my limbs. I love him dearly. He is my flesh and
> blood.... It is only because of God's promise to protect

God's promise...
Genesis 21:13.

> Ishmael, guaranteeing his survival and ensuring his future,
> that I can even begin to think about sending him off with
> Hagar into the desert. If I give them enough water and pro-
> visions, I know they can get to an oasis. Perhaps there they
> will find shelter and a place to settle. If it isn't too far, I might

visit Ishmael...
See the many
midrashim that
speak of Abraham
visiting Ishmael and
Hagar; in particular,
Sefer ha-Yashar,
Vayera, 41aff.

> even be able to visit Ishmael from time to time, though I
> wouldn't dare tell Sarah. I will never stop loving him; I can
> never cast him off.[30] After all, he's my son.

Perhaps Abraham convinced himself that it was in his
people's best interest to make it clear that Isaac was the
one who stood in the line of inheritance and who bore the
Divine imprimatur. Yet, Abraham knew in his heart that
banishing Ishmael and Hagar was simply wrong and that it
ran against everything that he felt in his gut. If he could
argue with God at Sodom and Gomorrah for the lives of
human beings whom he did not even know, then he surely
could have expressed more than a gesture of displeasure
when he was asked to be an accomplice to what might be
the murder of his son.[31] He hearkened to the Voice telling
him to cast off his son, all the while feeling that it was not
in the nature of a parent to act in this way. Perhaps by com-
plying with the call, which he thought was what God

wanted, he would demonstrate how far he was willing to go in his faithfulness to his God. Simply, it was a matter of a choice between human love and Divine will. It was an issue of his ego and the need to show Sarah and his people the sacrifice he was willing to make. At that moment, Isaac's fate was sealed, since the one question that was haunting Abraham (and God) had to be whether Abraham was also willing to sacrifice the son upon whom everything *rested*, the son who guaranteed his own future.[32]

Since so much rested upon Isaac,[33] it was Isaac whom Abraham loved the most, for Isaac embodied his dreams of future glory.[34] Therefore, it was Isaac who had to be the object of Abraham's greatest test: Could he sacrifice Isaac and demonstrate the extent of his fidelity to the Divine?[35] As with most young people, Abraham's faith—his mettle—had to be confirmed once more through some kind of ritual test.

Soon after the banishment of Ishmael, Abraham thought he heard God's Voice calling to him one more time, simply calling his name.[36] Though he had no idea what God wanted of him, he now understood the demands that being in relationship imply, and he responded accordingly: "*Hineini*," "Here I am." The task had not been defined, but Abraham demonstrated his developing maturity by responding to the call and showing his willingness to act. And he heard the Voice telling him: "Take your son, your favored one, Isaac, and go to the land of Moriah and offer him there as an offering on one of the heights which I will point out to you."

But was it really the call of the Divine that Abraham heard? Jacob knew exactly what Abraham must have been thinking. Many times in his own life, he, too, had felt unworthy of the gifts and blessings that the Divine had bestowed upon him: Why should he have been chosen by

calling his name...
Genesis 22:1.

Take your son...
Genesis 22:2.

God to lead this people called Israel? How had he shown that he deserved God's beneficence, especially the progeny that were given to him? As Jacob thought of his sons, in particular Joseph, and now his grandchildren whom he was about to bless, he could empathize with his grandfather's doubts:

I simply don't deserve...
Based on a *midrash* in Bereshit Rabbah 55:6.

I simply don't deserve the blessing of receiving a son in my old age, and I surely have not expressed to God my utter gratitude. How can I begin to show God how grateful I am for all that has been given me over the years, from the time I left Ur and started on this momentous journey? Time and again, I have survived and even flourished because of God's love for me. How do I convince the Divine of my loyalty and my willingness to sacrifice anything for the sake of God's name in the world?[37]

The Voice impelled Abraham to take his son to the land of Moriah and offer him as a sign of his fidelity to God. Abraham was not sure that this was really God's will. Could this really be what God wanted of him? Like other young people, he was not sure where he was going, but he was hopeful that it would become clear to him along the way. Only by setting forth on the journey, by confronting the range of his emotions, could he gain insight into himself and what was expected of him. By starting out for Moriah, he hoped he would be better able to discern the place for which he was destined.[38] Until he reached the mountain, he would have to live with this uncertainty. This, too, would be a test of his maturity.

The three-day journey to Moriah was fraught with pain and indecision on Abraham's part.[39] At times, he simply felt lost.[40] Determined, however, to prove his faith, he trudged along despite his exhaustion until he finally raised his eyes and saw a mountain in the distance. He knew that his

he finally raised his eyes...
Genesis 22:4.

moment of destiny was at hand. Having grown through life's experiences, a more mature Abraham was able to discern his destination without explicit instructions. He no longer needed God to describe it in detail.[41] He knew that this was the place of the sacrifice through which he would prove himself to God.

Abraham's zealousness was most evident when he and Isaac arrived at the site of the offering. He did all the work himself: building an altar, laying the wood upon it, and binding his son. Abraham was so self-involved that he acted like an automaton. There was absolutely no sign of emotion, though he was about to take his son's life. All we see is Abraham, the knight of faith, bent on proving himself by fulfilling what he perceived to be God's wish.

building an altar...
Genesis 22:9.

Abraham was so intent on making this sacrifice that he was oblivious to the fact that it was his *ben zekunim*, the child of his old age, the child for whom he had longed, whom he had bound upon the altar. At that moment, realizing that Abraham would actually kill Isaac, God implored the archangel Michael: "Why are you standing there? Don't you see that he's going to kill the boy? This cannot happen!" Michael tried to argue with God, saying that he did not have the power to stop Abraham, but God pushed the angel out of heaven, and Michael called out, "Abraham!" But Abraham did not hear the angel's desperate cry, and Michael had to call out a second time, "Abraham, lay not your hand upon the boy." Still bent on proving his fidelity, Abraham responded, "I won't touch him with my hands, but let me just take the knife and draw some blood. Please, let me do something!" But the angel insisted: "Don't do anything to the boy." Abraham would not yield: "God commanded me to slaughter Isaac, and you say not to slaughter him. The words of the teacher and the words of the disciple—to whom shall I hearken?" Finally,

implored the archangel...
This is a reworking of a *midrash* on Genesis 22:11–12, which is found in Midrash Va-Yosha.

God intervened and called out to Abraham: "I swear to you…because you have done this thing and not withheld your son." Only then did Abraham relent.

The sacrifice God wanted on the mountain that day was not Isaac. What Abraham had to sacrifice was his ego, the "I," so that he could hear God's true call.[42] Like other young people, Abraham had to transcend himself and move beyond his own ego needs to become the person he truly could be. Abraham started out on the journey to the land of Moriah to find God's place. In the end, he found his son. And he found himself.[43]

called to Abraham…
Genesis 22:15–18.

God then called to Abraham a second time and blessed him. Having finally passed the real test—sacrificing his own needs for what God truly wanted—Abraham was now ready to become a vehicle for God's work among the nations. God then blessed him by saying: "All the nations of the earth shall be blessed through your descendants, because you have hearkened to My voice."

All the nations…
Genesis 22:18.

Changing Priorities: Reaching Beyond Ourselves

As Jacob thought about Abraham's moment of encounter with God on Mount Moriah he couldn't help but recall his moment of destiny on the shore of the Jabbok. On that night, in a dream perhaps, he struggled with a man who looked like his brother Esau, though he also appeared quite angelic. Jacob came away from that encounter wholly changed. He seemed to have found himself as he confronted the Other in his life. Abraham, too, matured greatly as a result of the events on Mount Moriah. Awakened by the piercing call of his name, he recognized his essential self and what was important for the first time—and he left the mountain a different person.

shore of the Jabbok…
Genesis 32:23–33.

The change in Abraham was evident in the great emotion he exhibited when Sarah died. Returning to Be'er

Sarah died…
Genesis 23:1–2.

Sheva, he learned that Sarah had relocated her tents to Kiryat Arba while he was away, and had died there.[44] Abraham traveled to Kiryat Arba to mourn for her, shedding tears as he never had before:[45]

> I loved her more than anything else in the world, but I don't know if she ever realized it. Perhaps I didn't know it until it was too late. We never really talked. When we did, we always seemed to wind up angry at each other.... Truth be told, it was my fault. I did not know how to communicate my feelings to her, or for that matter to anyone in my family. They couldn't have known how much I cared for them, especially since I always spent so much time away from them doing what God expected of me. Now she is gone, and all I can do is try to find a fitting burial place for her.

The irony, of course, is that Abraham was closer to Sarah in death than he had ever been in life. A maturing Abraham, following the fearful trial on Mount Moriah and his bereavement after Sarah died, desperately needed a physical sign—even if it was a grave site—that would guarantee his future. Although he remembered the promises that God had made to him and to his descendants, for the first time he actually took possession of a portion, a small portion, of the promised land. He paid the full price for the Cave of Machpelah in Hebron, thus ensuring that it would be his in perpetuity.

paid the full price... Genesis 23:13–20.

But we see other signs of Abraham's transformation. Following Sarah's death, he recognized the fleeting nature of human existence and what is important in life, especially the relationship with others, with whom we share our lives. As a result, Abraham, who would have taken his son's life if the angel hadn't intervened, went to great lengths to find the right wife for Isaac. He sent his servant, Eliezer, on the arduous journey back to Aram Naharaim so Isaac could marry a woman from his own tribe. Abraham finally

He sent... Genesis 24.

understood not only his responsibility to perpetuate their line but also his own role as a father. Perhaps he even felt that, by doing so, he would gain even greater personal satisfaction than he had gotten from all of his actions on behalf of the God with whom he had a covenant.

Following Sarah's death, Abraham felt the pain of being alone. The pain was even more acute after Isaac took Rebecca as his wife. It was so severe that Abraham wanted to marry again. A mature Abraham realized that his happiness depended upon becoming one with another person. He traveled to Be'er Lahai Roi, where he had heard that Hagar had settled,[46] and he took her as his wife.[47] Abraham could now see Hagar differently. Emerging from his self-centered search for his identity, Abraham was now willing to fuse his identity with that of another person. He was finally ready for intimacy, ready to commit himself to a serious relationship and to develop the strength to live within such a commitment. All this implied some self-sacrifice. There was now room in his life to allow him to live with another. As a result, the Abraham we see now is remarkably different from his younger, less mature counterpart. He fathers six children with Hagar, and appears to be the archetypical family person who lives a happy, fulfilled life.

was even more acute...
B.T. Baba Kama 92b.

he took her...
See Bereshit Rabbah 61:4; Tanhuma Buber, Chayei Sarah 9; and Pirkei d'Rabbi Eliezer, Chapter 30, on Genesis 25:1.

six children...
Genesis 25:2.

CHAPTER SIX

ISAAC

The Young Adult

Erik Erikson: Stage Six
Intimacy vs. Isolation

- This is a time to leave one's parents' home and create one's own family and share in the care of offspring.
- The individual is ready for intimacy, to fuse his or her identity with others, to commit to long-term affiliations and partnerships. This entails facing the fear of ego loss—sacrificing a part of the self for another and, in the process, finding oneself anew. It also entails living up to the expectations of the other.
- Some people, however, try to protect themselves by isolating themselves and trying to avoid contact with others.
- Values and ideals are shared with other human beings, even while one's own sense of meaning is established. This involves being able to develop a realistic perception of the other as a whole person, rather than idealizing the other.
- The individual begins to confront the tensions and polarities of life, such as the fear of aging that results from losing a parent or discrepancies between aspirations and the realities of existence. Such a confrontation also entails facing real issues about the meaning of life.

In his musings, Jacob couldn't help but think about his father, Isaac, and the trauma that he'd experienced, which remained with him his entire life. Jacob understood how a person's life could change dramatically as a result of one fateful moment. Even in his own eventful life, the struggle with the faceless stranger on the banks of the Jabbok, which now seemed like a lifetime ago, had most altered his existence. Limping away from that confrontation, he knew that his life would never be the same and that his relationship with everyone he loved would be different. Isaac, too, though he might not have realized it immediately, experienced an utter transformation that fateful day on Mount Moriah.

Recognizing Our Parents, Discovering Ourselves

Isaac walked quietly alongside Abraham, trusting that his father knew where he was going and how to get there. Even though he was now a young adult, it seemed that Isaac meekly followed his father.[1] They walked together on the road to the mountain, Isaac relying on his father as a child depended upon his parent. Yet, as he carried the wood, he occasionally reached out to support his father, who faltered every few steps. At one point, he turned to his father and spoke, his words belying his age:

They walked together...
Genesis 22:6, 8.

> Father, everything seems prepared for the offering. We have cut sufficient wood for even a large animal, and we remembered the flintstone. But where is the ram for the offering? Where can we even find a ram in these hills? I don't understand why we didn't bring an animal with us. We always do.

Father...
Based on
Genesis 22:7.

As if he were a very young boy, Isaac not only was naively oblivious to his father's intentions, but seemed to be totally submissive. He was like the ram being led to the slaughter. Yet, his near sacrifice surely had a drastic and permanent effect upon Isaac. We can imagine the disillu-sionment, pain, and rejection he must have felt as the slaughtering knife was about to fall upon him. Years later, Jacob could also hear Isaac's words:

> The way to the top of the mountain was rugged, and we climbed it with considerable difficulty. When we reached the top of the mountain, I unloaded the kindling wood that father had put on my back, and he took the flint and the slaughtering knife. "But where is the lamb for the offering?" I asked in wonderment. My father remained silent for a moment. Then he said, "Adonai will select the lamb for the offering." "Adonai? I don't understand. What does Adonai have to do with this?" My father said hesitantly, "My son . . ." It seemed painful for him to say even that. His voice seemed to break. And then I finally understood. No...I did not real-ly understand. But this much I know. My father seized me and brought me to the heap of wood. He bound my hands and feet tightly. My eyes stared wide, desperately wide. His eyes were glassy and without expression. I began to stammer, "Adonai! Adonai! Adonai?" I cried. My father unsheathed the knife, and it came closer and closer. "Adonai," I cried out, "Master of the Universe, where are You?" My father placed the blade to my throat. "What are you doing? Are you crazy? I don't want to die. Let me go! Let me go, I tell you!"
>
> Father is now dead, and his death does not pain me in the least. On the contrary, I am almost glad that it happened. I cannot believe that he would have killed me if the angel had not intervened. From that moment on, there was only silence between us. I never spoke another word to him. I always saw him standing there with the knife in his hand...ready to kill me.[2]

At the denouement of the episode, Isaac was awakened to the fragility of life and to his father's true nature. He was no longer the naive young person who thought that his father could do no wrong and in whom Isaac had total confidence, assuming that his judgment and his ability to protect his son were impeccable. He now saw Abraham as a human being, with the same frailties as every other person. In discovering his father's humanness, he discovered himself. This was a powerful moment of maturation for Isaac, as it is for every young adult who witnesses his or her parents' frailty for the first time. Isaac would never be the same. The mark of this experience would remain with him throughout his entire life. What he had seen and felt would shape his whole being.[3]

The Isaac who ascended Mount Moriah with his father did not come down from the mountain.[4] A more mature, wiser Isaac descended in his place—one who, having experienced a near-death trauma at the hand of his father, was no longer umbilically connected to him. Isaac had become an individual in his own right. The irony is that, though he escaped Nothingness only because of the angel's intervention, and he realized his own mortality for the very first time, Isaac was finally liberated.[5]

Ready for Relationships: Creating New Ties with Family

Jacob could imagine what had happened to Isaac after the events on Mount Moriah. He pictured Isaac remaining on the mountaintop for a long while, unable to descend with his father. In the end, he refused to return home, though he would miss his mother greatly, choosing rather to settle in the Negev, away from Abraham. Living near Be'er Lahai Roi, Isaac strolled in the fields every afternoon as the sun was setting. As he walked by himself he couldn't help but think about his father and what could have happened on the mountain. He also conjured up visions of his mother,

strolled in the fields...
Genesis 24:62–63.

Sarah, who had recently died, and even of his step-brother, Ishmael, and Ishmael's mother, Hagar.

> I am literally alone in the world. My mother is dead, and I couldn't even bring myself to go to Hebron for her burial.[6] I simply could not face my father. I haven't seen him since our trek to the top of Moriah. As for Ishmael and Hagar, we heard from some travelers that they had settled near Be'er Lahai Roi, but I've had no contact with them. I actually wouldn't mind seeing them, since I have some wonderful memories of how Ishmael and I played together, even though he was much older than I. And though my mother often cautioned me about Hagar, and how she really didn't care for anyone or anything but Ishmael, I always felt that she was a good, warm person. Wouldn't it be something if I found them and they wound up as the only family I really have!

A vulnerable, lonely Isaac found himself near Hagar and Ishmael, two links to his fragile past. Perhaps his settling in the part of the Negev where they were living was intentional. How meaningful was it that Isaac decided, even if unconsciously, to live in the place where Hagar had fled after Sarah mistreated her before she gave birth to Ishmael?[7]

the place...
Genesis 16:14.

But why would he settle near Hagar and Ishmael if not to reestablish their relationship? Or was there more?

> When I think about it now, I know that I surely came to Be'er Lahai Roi to find Hagar and Ishmael, and through that renewed relationship to reconstruct my past. Perhaps I even hoped that Hagar had not remarried after she was banished from my father's house. Though I harbored many ill feelings toward my father because of what he had done to me, I still wanted to see him happy. Maybe if he felt complete in himself, there finally would be room in his life for me. And so I found myself in Be'er Lahai Roi with the intent to bring

Hagar back to my father, or at least make her aware that my mother had died and that my father was all alone and in desperate need of companionship.[8]

Falling in Love: Finding Ourselves through Another

Isaac may have been thinking about Ishmael and Hagar and his father as he walked in the field toward evening as was his custom, but little did he know that his entire life was about to change. For his father, Abraham, had sent his servant Eliezer back to the family home in Aram Naharaim, to Laban's house, to find a suitable wife for him, and he was about to meet his intended bride. Looking up, Isaac saw a camel caravan approaching. As it drew closer the woman riding on one of the lead camels raised her eyes, and their eyes met. She nearly fell off the camel with excitement, and he was so startled that he couldn't utter a word, though many thoughts raced though his mind:[9]

She nearly fell...
Genesis 24:64.

> I cannot believe my eyes. Is that Eliezer? What is he doing here? I haven't seen him since the day I set out with my father on the road to the Land of Moriah. And who is this woman with Eliezer? Could it be that my father asked Eliezer to find a wife for me? She is absolutely beautiful. I cannot take my eyes off of her. I know she realizes that I'm looking at her...she's covering her face with a veil. I hope I haven't embarrassed her.

covering her face...
Genesis 24:65.

Although Isaac's father and mother had lived together for many years and gone through many life experiences together, he could never remember that they had expressed to each other any of the feelings he now felt. Perhaps that is the way of children: they are, for the most part, oblivious to any romantic expressions between their parents. Yet, he was sure that his father had never felt this way about his mother. As much as Sarah had been Abraham's life partner, Abraham had never described her as beautiful. Isaac thought that he was the first person to have ever fallen hopelessly in love—and at first sight, no less.[10] He did take Rebekkah as his wife, and he indeed loved her deeply.

Until the moment that he met Rebekkah, Isaac felt alone in the world, since he was totally detached from his father. Worst of all, his mother was dead and could no longer give him the comfort and love that he so desperately needed. But Isaac wasn't paralyzed by his circumstances, and his response to Rebekkah demonstrated his growth and maturity. He could move beyond his pain and angst over Sarah's death, realizing that another human being could not only provide the necessary solace but also bring him to a new place in his life. In his love for Rebekkah, Isaac found a way to recreate his mother's care, devotion, and tenderness while gaining a fuller measure of wholeness in himself.[11] It was as if his mother were still alive and her presence could still be felt.[12] But there was more. Isaac felt closer to God than he had in quite some time. As a result of his experience on Mount Moriah and his mother's death immediately thereafter, Isaac felt that God had abandoned him—as if he were no longer in touch with the Divine presence. But in that moment when he gazed upon Rebekkah for the first time, and surely when he took her into his tent and made her his wife, God's presence was palpable. She gave meaning to his life.

The closeness between them, and the deep love and concern that Isaac had for Rebekkah, were quite evident in his actions. Jacob was almost embarrassed when he thought of this, for he couldn't help but compare his response to his wife, Rachel, with that of Isaac toward his beloved. It was difficult for Jacob to recall how he had

did take Rebekkah...
Genesis 24:65.

her presence...
Midrash Ha-Gadol
to Genesis 24:67.

abandoned him...
Based on Bereshit
Rabbah 60:16.

Rachel when she appeared...
Genesis 30:2.

chastised and cast blame on Rachel when she appeared to be barren, yet his father had been so supportive of Rebekkah in her anguish. For that matter, his grandfather, Abraham, had not responded to Sarah in any more loving way than he had to Rachel. In fact, his father, Isaac, stood out as an example of compassion as he prayed to God on behalf of Rebekkah. By contrast, neither he nor Abraham had raised his voice to the Divine in a similar way:

Sovereign of the Universe...
Based on Bereshit Rabbah 63:5.[13]

Sovereign of the Universe, may it be Your will that all the progeny You will grant me be from this righteous woman. From the first moment that I saw her, I knew that we were destined to be life partners. You had seen to it that our lives would merge and that from our union would emerge the future of our people. I couldn't think of having children with anyone but Rebekkah. Please, dear God, open her womb and make her fertile.

Isaac loved Rebekkah and was deeply committed to her. In fact, in contrast to the relationships of his ancestors and his sons, they were the only totally lifelong monogamous couple.[14]

Isaac's affection for Rebekkah was even evident when it was least expected. Living near Gerar, among the

Isaac feared...
Genesis 26:6–9.

Philistines, Isaac feared that Rebekkah's beauty would result in his being killed. As Abraham had with Sarah at Gerar, he concocted the ruse that Rebekkah was his sister, hoping that would insure his safety. Isaac seemed to fall back to the same adolescent behavior exhibited by his father, Abraham, in which he presumed that the Philistines were his enemies and that they would covet his wife, even though they had done nothing to warrant being thought of in this manner.

Young people tend to see perfectly well-meaning individuals as their adversaries. The inappropriateness of

Isaac's actions was evident when Avimelech, the king of Gerar, said, "So she is your wife! Why then did you say 'She is my sister'? What have you done to us? One of the people might have lain with your wife, and you would have brought guilt upon us."

Ironically, the ruse was discovered when Isaac was seen acting fondly toward Rebekkah.[15] Even when he thought that his life was on the line, he couldn't restrain his love and passion for her. Isaac certainly had come a long way from the days when he felt totally alone after his trauma on Mount Moriah. That he had grown tremendously was evidenced by his ability to give himself to another.

Setting Down Roots: Living among Strangers

Unlike his father, Isaac put down roots in the Land of Canaan, the land that God had promised to his people in perpetuity. He sowed the land, planted extensive crops, and established his family in Philistine territory. He accumulated so much wealth that his Philistine neighbors were very envious. Isaac was upset when he heard that his neighbors, in an effort to drive him from the land, had begun to stop up the wells that Abraham had dug:

sowed the land... Genesis 26:12–14.

> I simply can't believe that Avimelech and his people are trying to drive us from the land that we've settled and planted. Nothing has really changed since the days of my father. Our people are still fighting with our neighbors over water rights. What are we to do? My heart tells me to respond as my father did—to stand up to Avimelech and fight for what is right. Otherwise, people will think that my passivity means I am a coward. However, my goal always has been to live in peace. We must be concerned first and foremost with our survival; we cannot confront our neighbors directly.

the days of my father... Genesis 21:25–34, where Abraham argued with Avimelech over a well that had been inappropriately seized.[16]

While a more aggressive posture might have appeared to be heroic, it most probably would have resulted in the decimation of Isaac's people.[17] However, even though the people of Gerar quarreled with him over each well that he dug, which raised his anger to the point of naming the wells Esek and Sitnah, meaning "contention" and "harassment," Isaac kept moving his encampment until he uncovered a well that was not contested. He called it Rehovot, saying, "Now at last God has granted us ample space to increase in the land." By doing this Isaac showed a great deal of maturity. As a result, he not only survived but also gained the respect of Avimelech and his people.

Nevertheless, when Avimelech came to him from Gerar, Isaac was not afraid to pointedly respond to the king of the Philistines:

> Why have you now come to me, after having driven me from the land? After what you and your people have done, I would have expected that you would be the last person I would lay eyes upon. I have tried to avoid any confrontation between us, and have finally found a place to dwell that seems far away from any of your camps. I will not move again.

As a result of the way Isaac had acted, the Philistines saw what type of person he was and that God surely was with him, so they signed a pact with him, in which each party pledged to live in peace with the other. Ironically, the same day that they exchanged oaths, Isaac's men dug a well that turned out to be an excellent water source. Isaac named it Sheva. To this day, the place is most appropriately called Be'er Sheva, "the Seven Wells" or "the Well of the Oath."

Isaac, because of the mature manner in which he dealt with his Philistine neighbors, ensured the survival of his people and that they would have a future. On the surface it appeared as though Isaac had simply followed in his

the people of Gerar quarreled...
Genesis 26:17–21.

He called it...
Genesis 26:22.

Why have you come...
Based on Genesis 26:27.

they signed a pact...
Genesis 26:28–33.

father's footsteps, not only in his confrontation with Avimelech but in redigging the very wells that Abraham had dug. It also seems that he had a very difficult time differentiating himself from his powerful father.[18] However, even in this instance, he also showed himself to be different from Abraham. In his search for water and sustenance, he began by redigging the same wells that his father had dug. He even gave them the same names his father had used. Isaac knew that he was an heir to Abraham's legacy. He was linked to the past and couldn't avoid it. Yet, even though at first he uncovered his father's wells, he not only reconfigured his father's wells but located his own water sources. The past was very much a part of him, though he was able to successfully assert his own power and independence.[19]

redigging...
Genesis 26:18.

Creating a Family: Learning How to Raise Children

At first glance, Isaac's relationship with Rebekkah and with his two sons seemed to show a lack of maturity. It appears that he was embroiled in a complicated battle with his wife for the affection of Jacob and Esau. It is true that parents occasionally use their relationships with their children to compensate for the emotional disappointments in their marriage. Isaac and Rebekkah's marriage may not have been any different. Perhaps their attachments to different sons was a substitute for spousal companionship; each was able to create a primary emotional bond with one of their children.[20] Jacob was a quiet homebody and evoked in Rebekkah feelings of love and protectiveness. He was the more vulnerable one, the most needy of the siblings, and he became the object of her affection. In contrast, Isaac had strong feelings for their son Esau, though it seems strange that he was drawn to his firstborn son.

homebody...
Genesis 25:27–28.

As Jacob lay waiting for Joseph and his sons to appear he thought about his father's relationship with his brother. Even though he had eventually received his father's blessing, he couldn't help but wonder why Isaac loved Esau more:

When I think about my father and brother, I'm still mystified by their relationship. They always seemed so completely opposite. My father was mild-mannered, even somewhat passive, while Esau was an active, virile sportsman. Truth be told, my father and I were almost identical, and Esau was his total opposite. Perhaps he was drawn to Esau because of this very fact. He loved him because Esau possessed qualities that he himself did not have. Through his relationship with Esau, he could vicariously live a different type of existence; he could become the strong hunter, the man of the outdoors upon whom others are dependent. But I think there is more. I think that Esau reminded my father of his long-lost brother, Ishmael, who like Esau was a man of the field, wild and impetuous. Drawing close to Esau allowed Isaac to overcome in part the guilt and the loneliness he must have felt after Ishmael was banished from their house.[21]

The rather unfortunate gravitation of Isaac to Esau, and Rebekkah to Jacob, caused hatred between the siblings. Yet, Isaac's feelings for Esau were probably very honest. Isaac favored him because Esau cared for him and provided for the family. Not only did Isaac develop a taste for the game that Esau brought home, but he knew he could count on his son to be there for him. He needed the fidelity of his son—the reassurance that he would not be alone as he grew older. Perhaps all this was the result of the horrible memories Isaac still harbored of the experience on Mount Moriah and his own father's abandonment of him.

Isaac truly loved Esau and wanted to demonstrate to him how much he meant to him. Esau deserved nothing

taste for the game...
Genesis 25:28.

less. After all, this was the son who cared for him and would be there for him in his old age. How could he not give him his innermost blessing?

Esau, my son, I am not a youngster anymore. I do not know how long God will allow me to enjoy this life. But one thing I do know is how much you give to me: your selfless devotion and loyalty. Please, take your gear and hunt some game, and prepare it just the way I love. Bring it to me so that we can eat together. Then I will give you my blessing. So often you have been my support, doing all that I have needed. It is now time for me to give to you that which you deserve as my first-born son: to reciprocate your affection and love.

Esau, my son...
Based on
Genesis 27:1–4.

Yet, even though Isaac loved Esau in a special way, he was responsive to both his sons. This was most evident in the events that unfolded regarding Isaac's blessing. After Esau had gone off to hunt game for his father's meal, Rebekkah, knowing that it was Jacob who was destined to receive the blessing, prepared food, gave Jacob Esau's clothing to wear, and placed the animal skins on his arms and neck so that he could take Esau's place before his father. So when Jacob, dressed as his brother and carrying the food that his mother had prepared, approached his father, a seemingly confused Isaac said to him, "*Hineini* [here I am]. Who are you, my son?" Isaac did not ask which son stood in front of him. This showed his willingness to be there for both of his children, not only for Esau. As a mature parent, he knew he had to give equally to both of them, irrespective of his more intense feelings for Esau. Isaac's ability as a parent was even more obvious when he said to Jacob, who was feigning to be Esau, "Who are you, my son?" Isaac challenged his child to look at himself honestly, to see himself for what he was. His question really was "What are you, my son? Who are you really?"

prepared food...
Genesis 27:14–17.

Hineini...
Genesis 27:18.

When Isaac challenged his son, it was clear that he knew that it was Jacob who had come for the blessing. Being sight-impaired, he naturally compensated for his disability by listening more intently; he had already heard Jacob's voice. "The voice [was indeed] the voice of Jacob." But all we have to do is to listen to how Isaac questioned Jacob to know that he recognized that it was not Esau who stood before him:

The voice...
Genesis 27:22.

> My son, I do not understand how you were able to hunt so quickly and then prepare the food. It seems that it took you no time to return.... Come closer so that I can touch you, my son. Are you really my son Esau or not? The voice is the voice of Jacob, but the hands are the hands of Esau. Are you really my son Esau? Come close and kiss me, my son.

My son, I do not...
Based on
Genesis 27:20–26.

But there were other, even more telling signs that made it easy for Isaac to understand which son should receive his blessing. According to the dowry he had given Rebekkah when they married, Isaac had to provide her with two goats each day. The goat skins Jacob wore as well as the food Rebekkah had prepared, in contrast to the venison that Esau hunted, indicated to Isaac that this was Rebekkah's way of telling him that Jacob was chosen for the blessing. It was Jacob, then, of whom the oracle had spoken when the two brothers struggled in their mother's womb. Somehow God had a hand in the choice, which was also apparent the moment Isaac heard Jacob mention God's name, in response to his question about how he had succeeded so quickly in hunting and preparing the food: "Because the Lord your God granted me good fortune."

the dowry...
Bereshit
Rabbah 65:14.

of whom the oracle...
Genesis 25:23.
was also apparent...
Bereshit
Rabbah 65:19.

the Lord your God...
Genesis 27:20.

Isaac was fully aware of the deception, yet he never raised the issue with either Jacob or Rebekkah. He realized that Jacob had to receive the blessing, no matter how much he loved Esau. Isaac had become convinced, when Esau married two Hittite women, that Esau could not be trusted to lead the people after his death. This had upset Isaac and Rebekkah terribly, and they understood that Esau did not take the survival of their people seriously enough.[22]

married two Hittite women... Genesis 26:34.

A mature Isaac had to make the most difficult decision of his life. As the leader of the tribe he knew that the spiritual destiny of his people hung in the balance, and which son would receive the blessing was crucial.

But this could not diminish the pain he felt, which is evident when we hear him getting ready to confront Esau as he returned from hunting:

It's done. It had to be this way. As much as I love Esau and value his loyalty and feelings, he is not the son to lead our people. He simply does not have the qualities that would guarantee our people's survival and prosperity in the difficult times ahead. To be sure, there are things about Jacob that have always bothered me, especially his reserved nature and at times his lack of emotion. Yet, from his birth, it was clear that he was destined for this moment.

Each of my sons deserves blessing, and I shall also bless Esau. But the blessings need to be appropriate to each child. If only it could be different. I wish Esau could take over for me and lead our family. But it is not meant to be. How can I possibly face him? What words can I say that will diminish the hurt and lessen his feelings of betrayal and rejection? What words can a father say to a son who had counted on the father's blessing and who thought that he rightfully deserved it?

He's coming. I can hear the heaviness of his steps outside…. Esau, is that you? Then who was it who hunted the game and brought it to me?[23] I can't believe it! I ate the food he prepared, and I blessed him! What can I say? What's done is done. That blessing cannot be taken away. Your brother came to me with guile. He tricked me. He stole the blessing. But I will bless you, too.

Esau, is that you... Based on Genesis 27:32–33.

Although Isaac made the choice that had to be made, he was deeply disturbed by what he had done. Like every loving parent, he found it painful to admit that since the child he loved the most had certain limitations, he could not give him what he desired. Unfortunately, Isaac could not bear the responsibility for his own actions, and he blamed Jacob for them. By doing this, he hoped to minimize Esau's hatred of him. And in blaming Jacob, he exacerbated the already fragile relationship between the brothers, demonstrating for all that he had matured, he still had much to work on in terms of his own growth.

Giving a Blessing: Pointing to the Future

Though Jacob still felt guilty because of what he had done to Esau, he also remembered how it felt to have his father lay his hands upon him and bless him. It was a turning point in his life. He felt whole and protected, and he knew that he would succeed no matter what happened to him. It was Isaac's way of ensuring his future by enveloping Jacob not only with a sense of safety and caring but also with a guarantee of protection.[24] If he concentrated hard enough, Jacob probably could still feel his father's touch. As he anticipated blessing his grandchildren, he knew how much it would mean to them and the significance it would have for their lives.

Jacob knew that his father had been the first parent to utter words of blessing to his progeny. He could not recall any stories about his grandfather Abraham, nor about any earlier heroes, who had blessed their children. And Jacob knew how powerful such words could be.

But the irony was this: Jacob knew that the blessing his father may have originally intended for his brother was not the most significant blessing he received. The first blessing

first blessing...
Genesis 27:28–29.

did promise him material wealth and guaranteed his physical survival. But it was the words that his father spoke to him before his hasty departure for his uncle Laban's house that carried the greatest consequence. At Rebekkah's urging that Jacob not marry foreign women as his brother Esau had, Isaac sent for Jacob and instructed him and blessed him again at one and the same time:

> Jacob, your mother and I are very concerned about your future and the future of our people. If you stay here in Canaan, it is inevitable that you will marry from among the daughters of our neighbors. Then what will happen to our family? How will we ever maintain our identity on this land that God has promised to us through my father, Abraham? My son, you shall not take a wife from among the Canaanite women. Prepare immediately to leave for your mother's family in Paddan-aram, and marry from among the daughters of her brother Laban. Only in this way will you enjoy the legacy of Abraham.
>
> May El Shaddai bless you and make you fertile and numerous. May God grant you and your offspring the blessing of Abraham, that you may return to this land, which God gave to our ancestors, and possess it.

Jacob, your mother...
Based on
Genesis 28:1–4.

The blessing that linked Jacob to the past and guaranteed his future possession of the land of Canaan would be his if he and his descendants continued to be a distinct nation covenanted to the God of Abraham. The instruction that Isaac gave to Jacob about marrying one of Laban's daughters was an integral part of the blessing.[25]

The blessings of future greatness came to Jacob when he retraced the journey of his grandfather, Abraham. Ironically, Jacob eventually inherited the land by leaving it and then returning to it from Haran, from Laban's house. Unlike his father Isaac, who never departed from Canaan,

Not only did Jacob...
Genesis 28:6–9.

Jacob would have to feel that he was a stranger in a strange land before he could find his home. Isaac, as a maturing, responsible parent, began to guide his children's lives, conveying the values by which they should live. Not only did Jacob listen to him, leaving immediately for his mother's family, but even Esau came to realize that marrying Canaanite women displeased his father, and he decided not to do it again. So he went to Ishmael and took Mahalat, his uncle's daughter, as a wife. In this way, Isaac began to provide a secure foundation for the future of his family. And he knew that Jacob and his children would surely be blessed.

CHAPTER SEVEN

THE YOUNG JACOB

Maturity

Erik Erikson: Stage Seven
Generativity vs. Stagnation

- Concern for others broadens, and a focus on the next generation begins. Self-concern is overcome in the process of guiding and helping one's progeny plan for their future.
- The parents' role is to support the separation and individuation of their children and to affirm their future. Over time, their role shifts from arbitrary authority to teacher and confidant.
- At a time in their lives when parents experience the death of their own parents and the departure of their children from home, and as other changes occur in their lives, they need to establish new emotional ties. In the process, they discover intergenerational connectedness.
- This stage is time to begin integrating the disparate forces in one's life and being, and also to develop a long-term vision, which involves the need to prepare one's children to succeed one's own generation.
- The danger is for the individual to regress to a stage of wanting to be cared for, rather than caring for others. Another danger is to succumb to the desire to be dependent on one's children.

As Jacob thought about the blessings he would bestow upon his twelve sons, thus ensuring their future as leaders of the people of Israel, he thought about his father and the blessings he and his brother Esau had received. Realizing the daunting responsibility that he now had to bless his own children, he could finally appreciate his father's difficulty in providing the appropriate blessings for both him and Esau.

His father's actions became crystal clear to him. After all the years of thinking that he had tricked his aging father into giving him the blessing of the firstborn at his mother's urging, Jacob saw Isaac in a different light. No longer could he think of him as someone who had been manipulated. His father had made a deliberate, calculated decision about who would best lead his people. Never intending to hurt Esau, he had blessed both his sons. Jacob received the blessing that his father had received from Abraham, while Esau was blessed in his own right.

Isaac's Model: Blessing Both Sons

Jacob now knew that his father had feigned incapacity in order to ensure that he would steal the blessing originally meant for his brother. Isaac would live for many more years, which indicates that he had not been old and senile at the time of the dual blessings but had known about the deception and was a party to its outcome.[1] For Jacob to assert his own strength and independence, Isaac had no choice but to appear weak and easily manipulated. By giving up his authority, he entrusted the next generation with their people's future.[2] Jacob could best lead if his father was no longer in a position of leadership.

Jacob seemed to gain strength and power from his daring act of trickery. At the moment when he put on Esau's clothes and the animal skins that his mother provided for

Esau's clothes...
Genesis 27:15–16.

him, he was not merely dressing himself up as his brother. He was demonstrating that he really possessed the qualities that were so evident in Esau.

At first when my mother placed the animal skins on my arms and neck, and I put on Esau's clothes, I felt very strange. Nothing seemed to fit. The skins kept sliding off my arms, and I kept scratching my neck. I kept thinking that it just wasn't right to disguise myself as my brother. And besides, father would surely be able to tell the difference between the costume I was wearing and my brother's true nature. And he would curse me, not bless me.

curse me...
Based on
Genesis 27:11–12.

But soon I began to feel more comfortable. It was almost as if the clothes and the skins were meant for me. A strange sensation overcame me—it was as if a part of me that had been there, dormant all along, had now emerged. I felt as if a side of me had awakened at that moment. So when I carried the food mother had prepared into my father's tent, and he responded by asking, "Who are you, my son?" it seemed almost natural for me to say, without thinking, "I am Esau, your firstborn." At that moment, I truly felt like my brother.

Jacob was not only an introspective, quiet tent dweller. He was also virile, strong, and cunning. He was a man of the field. It was the combination of these characteristics, the very totality of his being, that justified his receiving his father's blessing.[3]

Although at first Esau hated his brother for once again taking what was rightfully his, he, too, was essentially changed by what Isaac had done. Hearing his father's cry and seeing his tears as he tried to explain what had happened, Esau realized the depth of his father's affection for him and the power of the blessing he had been given. Isaac had promised him that he would enjoy the fruits of his labors, that he would luxuriate in the fat of the land and the taste of the dew of heaven.

fat of the land...
Genesis 27:39.

And when Jacob left Canaan to live in Haran with Laban's family, Isaac gave Esau total charge of the family homestead, trusting him to care for the fields and the flocks and, in effect, letting him take his place as the head of the tribe. Though he had not been given the blessing of Abraham, Esau knew that his future was guaranteed and that he would never want for anything, including his father's love.

In a dream...
Genesis 28:11ff.

No sooner did Jacob depart from Be'er Sheva than he was able to discern *his* own identity and future. In a dream at Beth El, he envisioned a ladder that reached toward the heavens, with angels moving up and down upon it. He realized that he had experienced the presence of the God of his grandfather, Abraham, and of his father, Isaac. This confirmed that he stood in the covenantal chain and that he was heir to the promise of the Land of Canaan. Even though Jacob, before leaving for Haran, had heard from his father the scope of the blessings he would enjoy, he now personally intuited that only through him and his descendants would all the nations of the earth be blessed. He knew that God would be with him on his journey and that he would return one day to claim the land that had been promised to him. Like his father, Isaac, he was now ready to find love, create a family, and ensure the continuity of his people.

Loving Both Rachel and Leah: Jacob's Maturation

came to water...
Genesis 29:9ff.

Eliezer, who had been sent...
Genesis 24:10ff.

Jacob met the love of his life when Rachel came to water her father's flocks at a well in Haran. His mother had been chosen to be Isaac's wife at the same well.[4] Unlike Isaac, however, Jacob chose his wife for himself. Abraham's servant, Eliezer, who had been sent back to Aram Naharaim to find a suitable mate for Isaac, found her at the well outside the city. But Jacob encountered Rachel all by himself, and the moment they met he was overwhelmed and suffused with energy he had never experienced before.

As Jacob was talking with several shepherds at the well he was told that the daughter of his mother's brother, Laban, was approaching with her father's flock. When Jacob saw her face, he was overcome with emotion; the mere glimpse of her had transformed him. And although he was told by the shepherds that the stone covering the well could be rolled aside only when all the men worked together, the power that he felt at that moment prompted him to approach the well and remove the well stone by himself. This feat was clearly due to the effect that Rachel's appearance had upon him; he had the strength and the will to do anything for her.

stone covering the well... Genesis 29:8.

Please, let me water the flock for you. No...no...let me. Here, I'll pour the water into the trough so that the sheep can drink. Surely, you do not know who I am, but I am the son of your father's sister. I am Rebekkah's son, Jacob. It has been a long and arduous journey from Canaan, but I am so happy to see you. I was hoping that I could find your father's house easily. It must be God's doing that I should come to this well just when you would arrive to water your flock, Rachel. What can I say? I almost feel that I have come home.

do not know... Based on Genesis 29:10–12.

Jacob could not control his emotions. He reached out for Rachel's hand, drew her toward him, and kissed her.[5] Though a bit embarrassed, she returned his affection. It was all too much for Jacob. His tears began to flow as he raised his voice in gratitude to God for his good fortune. He had found his family and his future.

Indeed, Jacob loved Rachel from his first glance of her at the well. She was even more than he could have ever imagined. There was a specialness about her which

ever imagined... Based on Genesis 29:17.

transcended her physical characteristics, and he knew that she was the love of his life. In thinking about his father's love for his mother, which he had always thought was the result of his father's need for comfort and companionship following Sarah's death, Jacob realized that Isaac had never felt what he did for Rachel.[6] Perhaps it was the way of children to think that their parents could never feel anything as intensely as they did. Nevertheless, Jacob was simply consumed by his passion for Rachel, and he yearned to be with her.

In his eagerness to make Rachel his wife, he pledged to Laban to work for seven years to gain her hand in marriage. This would not be a hardship for him, because he knew that in the end she would be his forever. And indeed, the years seemed like only a few days as he anticipated their union, because he loved her so. But while Jacob found an idyllic love with Rachel, he came to learn that there was more to life and relationship than romance, if it was to last and be totally satisfying. Rachel's older sister, Leah, whom Laban deceptively substituted for Rachel on the night that Jacob was supposed to marry Rachel, taught him about another kind of relationship. Leah taught him to focus upon family and children. She taught him to be a more mature person. While Rachel was initially barren and could not join Jacob in creating a future, Leah was quite fertile and quickly gave birth to several sons. And even though Leah always felt unloved, knowing that Jacob desired Rachel more, the truth was that he did love her.

> Though my feelings for Leah are quite different from those for Rachel, in some ways I have come to appreciate her even more than her sister. Even Rachel understands how important Leah is to me. Sometimes she is clearly envious of Leah and our relationship, and I have little patience for her envy. The truth is that through my relationship with Leah I have learned about the complexities of life and what is most

a few days...
Genesis 29:20

Rachel was initially barren...
Genesis 29:31.

did love her...
Genesis 29:30.

envious of Leah...
Genesis 30:1.

important.[7] Though the spark that is evident when Rachel and I are together is missing between Leah and me, I realize that the power of my moments with Rachel last but briefly. In its place, I feel for Leah a sense of devotion and sharing that will bind us together forever. I think Leah understands this as well as I do, since the names she has given to several of our sons reflect her sense of our abiding relationship. When, for example, our third child was born, she named him Levi, saying, "This time my husband will be attached to me forever."[8]

named him Levi...
Genesis 29:34.

The love between Jacob and Leah grew over time. And when she died, he lamented her exceedingly, realizing what she had meant to him.[9] The final irony was that when Jacob died, he was buried next to her in the Cave of Machpelah, where his immediate ancestors were also buried, while Rachel, the object of his desire, was buried alone, on the road to Bethlehem, after dying unexpectedly in childbirth.

Jacob Builds for the Future

Nothing came easily for Jacob. He pledged to work for seven years in order to marry Rachel, and he worked hard. Why he offered to work for such a long time to gain the hand of Laban's daughter is hard to know. Perhaps he did not want Laban to ever claim that he had taken advantage of him. So, unlike his father and grandfather, Jacob had the experience of working for another person, of submitting to his demands, standards, and approval. Jacob experienced vulnerability as he learned how to depend on another person for his support. In the process, he quickly matured.

work for seven years...
Genesis 29:17.

But after fulfilling his pledge, he did not hesitate to demand what was rightfully his. We no longer see a quiet, passive Jacob when he blurted out to Laban, "Give me my

Give me...
Genesis 29:21.

wife, for my time is fulfilled, that I may consummate my marriage with her." And when Laban tricked him by substituting Leah for Rachel, he confronted Laban directly, claiming that he had been deceived. Perhaps he also finally learned what it meant to deceive another person, and he gained a new perspective on his own act of deception when he had tricked his father into thinking he was Esau:

How could you...
Based on Genesis 29:25ff.

How could you have done such a thing to me? I worked for you for seven long years so that I could marry Rachel, and now I find that I should not have trusted you. Seven years ago, I pledged myself to you with the confidence that you would reward my labors. And now, you deceive me?[10] What? You tell me that it is not the custom in your place to marry off the younger before the older! Why didn't you tell me this seven years ago? I never realized that the younger child could not take the place of the firstborn. How ironic! After gaining Esau's birthright for a pot of lentil soup and tricking my father into bestowing upon me the blessing intended for my brother, I wind up marrying Leah, your firstborn daughter.

Jacob served Laban for twenty years, fulfilling his promises to him and finally marrying Rachel as well. Yet, when his service was completed, Jacob did not hesitate to stand up to Laban, demanding that he be allowed to leave with his wives and children:

Now give me...
This passage is based on Jacob's remarks in Genesis 30:25ff.

Laban, I have served you well lo these many years. Now give me leave that I may return to my homeland with my wives and children, for whom I have labored on your behalf. You know well the valuable service that I have rendered to you, and how your livestock have fared under my hand. The little you possessed before I came here has grown to much, with God's blessings. And now, I must think of my own family and its future. I must make provision for my household.

Realizing that Laban would not give him what he so clearly deserved, Jacob made a deal with Laban in which he would settle for all the spotted sheep and goats, realizing that his father-in-law assumed he would take only a small portion of the flock. However, by crossbreeding the white and black animals, he was able to increase his own flocks and wealth inordinately. Jacob was now the head of a large family with many possessions. All this he accomplished on his own. He had come to Haran with only his staff and the clothes on his back, and now he was about to leave a wealthy man.[11] Jacob was surely a self-made individual, which perhaps sets him apart from his grandfather and father, each of whom had inherited wealth from the previous generation.[12]

deal with Laban... Based on Genesis 30:27–43.

When Jacob finally left Paddan-aram, with his family and possessions, Laban pursued him to retrieve what he felt belonged to him. Yet in the end, when Jacob stood up to his powerful father-in-law who had manipulated him all these years, Laban was stunned by what he heard and saw:

> Why do you pursue me? What is my crime that you should follow after us? During the twenty years I spent in your service, your ewes and she-goats never miscarried, and I never feasted upon the rams from your flock. That which was torn by beast I never brought to you; I myself made good the losses, which you exacted from me. In the fourteen years I served for your daughters and the six years I served for your flocks, you changed my wages time and time again. Had not the God of my ancestors been with me, you would have sent me away empty-handed!

Why do you pursue... Based on Genesis 31:36ff.

Jacob was no longer a powerless young refugee desperately searching for his own identity. Laban now confronted a mature, confident tribal head who had substance and mettle and was quite able to lead and provide for his own family.

Jacob Prepares to Claim His Rightful Position

Throughout his confrontation with Laban, Jacob emphasized that he believed God's will ensured his success. Over and over, he invoked the God of his fathers as the force that guaranteed that he would not leave Paddan-aram empty-handed:

the God of my fathers...
This is based on Genesis 31:5–9, 42.

> If the God of my fathers, the God of Abraham, and the Fear of Isaac had not been with me, you—Laban—would have deprived me of all that was due me and sent me away with nothing. But God noticed my plight and all the work that I have done these twenty years, and He has judged me kindly. God would not let you harm me. It is God Who ultimately gave me my reward; and God Who guaranteed me the flocks that I deserve.

A maturing Jacob was finally able to confront and internalize the beliefs and identity of his father and grandfather. He could relate to his father's mode of worship, which was evident when he referred to the "Fear of Isaac," the term used for Isaac's relationship with God, which perhaps had haunted him until that very moment.[13] Jacob also firmly recognized the role God played in his life, and he realized that what would happen to him would be part of a larger plan, which depended upon the Divine. And through a dream, Jacob also came to understand that part of God's intent was for him to return to his homeland and claim what was rightfully his.

I had a dream...
The paragraph is based on Genesis 28:18–22 and 31:13.

I had a dream in which an angel of God called to me, "Jacob!" and I answered, "Here I am." "I am the God of Beth El, where you anointed a pillar on your journey to Aram Naharaim and made a vow to me, saying, "If God remains with me, if God protects me on this journey that I am making...and if I return safely to my father's house, then the Lord shall indeed be my God. And this place, marked by the pillar that I have erected, shall be God's abode." Now, arise and leave this land and return to your own land, the land of your grandfather, Abraham, and your father, Isaac."

A maturing Jacob was now ready to return home and assume his mantle of leadership; he finally understood his covenantal responsibility and his place in the line that had begun with Abraham. But it took the birth of Joseph to make Jacob realize that the time had come for him to leave Laban and continue the journey of his life. For even though he now had ten sons, it was with Rachel's birthing of Joseph that the family was complete. They could now return to Jacob's homeland and begin to fulfill their national destiny, which God had predicted to Abraham many years before.

the birth of Joseph...
Genesis 30:25.

predicted...
Genesis 15:1–16.

Much time would pass, however, before Jacob and his family would actually settle in Canaan. It was almost as if the mere resolve to return was not enough, since coming home meant confronting his brother Esau, and dealing with all that troubled Jacob in his life. It meant reentering his father's domain and coming to grips with his relationship with Isaac, whom he had tricked and replaced, and whom he greatly loved and missed.

actually settle...
See Rashi's comment on Genesis 33:17, in which he quotes B.T. Megillah 17a.

The Journey Home: Jacob Becomes Whole

As he lay in his tent Jacob thought about those earlier days, and how he had felt when he left Laban's house, anticipating his return to Canaan. He recalled that during the arduous journey from Paddan-aram, he was flush with thoughts about his brother, and what would transpire when they finally met again. Would Esau still hate him and try to kill him? Could they ever overcome the chasm of animosity? What could they possibly say to each other?

As Jacob approached Canaan he became more and **more frightened**, and he divided his retinue into two camps, thinking that if Esau attacked one, the other could escape. For the first time in his life, he prayed to God. A mature Jacob was finally willing to admit his fears and recognize that he alone did not have the power to ensure his survival. Humbled by his fear of death, and feeling alone, Jacob looked to God for help:[14]

more frightened...
Genesis 32:8–9.

O God...
Based on Genesis 32:10ff.

O God and God of my grandfather, Abraham, and God of my father, Isaac, O Lord who said to me, "Return to your native land and I will deal bountifully with you," I am unworthy of all the kindness that you have steadfastly shown me.[15] Years ago, I left Canaan with nothing but my walking stick and backpack. I fled to Haran, not knowing if I would ever return home. I certainly could not have anticipated what would happen to me over the ensuing years. It was surely Your love and protection that not only guaranteed my survival of the difficulties I faced, but that made it possible for me to flourish. You have promised that my offspring will be as numerous as the sands of the sea. Now I must face my brother Esau, who surely harbors much hatred for me. Years ago, he swore to kill me. I fear that he will now carry out his pledge. He may even kill my wives and children, thereby avenging the injustice he feels that I committed against him. Deliver me, I pray, from the hand of my brother, from the hand of Esau.

In humbling himself before God, Jacob also realized that he could not defeat Esau in battle, and that the only possible way he could survive was to reconcile with him. As he realized his dependence on God for his life, so, too, would he have to ask Esau to treat him kindly. In one and the same moment, he had to come to both God and Esau as a servant comes to his master. And so he sent messengers to Esau bearing gifts of flocks. They were also directed to say to Esau:

> To my lord, Esau, I, your servant Jacob, have lived for a score of years with our uncle, Laban, in Haran, and now I have returned with all that I have acquired. I send these gifts to you in the hope of gaining your favor. I trust the years have enabled you to understand that I never wanted to hurt you, though I know the pain you must have felt all this time. You are my brother, and both of us have grown since the last time we saw each other. I return home with one hope: that we can live as brothers in peace. Please, find it in your heart to show me favor, and I pledge that I will be your faithful servant.

To my lord, Esau...
Based on Genesis 32:5–7 and 17–21.

The impending meeting with Esau, was, for Jacob, conditioned by his newly developing relationship with God. A mature Jacob finally understood that we come to a relationship with God through our relationship with other human beings, especially those closest to us. He also understood that an act against our brother or sister, against any other human being, is a sin against the Divine. By fearing Esau, Jacob's guilty conscience imbued his brother with divine power. Esau was perhaps a stand-in for God.[16]

stand-in for God...
Based on Genesis 33:10, in which Jacob says to his brother, "To see your face is like seeing the face of God."

Crossing the Jabbok: Jacob Integrates His Life

Jacob knew in the deep recesses of his being that meeting Esau would represent the final step in facing himself. No matter what precautions he might take to prepare for this, no matter how many gifts he could send ahead to his brother to propitiate him, the moment of confrontation was about to come, and it involved more than seeing Esau again. For Jacob, that moment would be one of ultimate vulnerability: He would have to face himself and who he had become.

For all his defensive posturing, Jacob found himself alone on the bank of the Jabbok River. For some unknown reason, he had sent his family and all his possessions across the river while he remained alone on the other side. It was there, at *Ma'avar Yabbok*, at the point of crossing the river, whose letters were simply an inversion of Jacob's own name, *Ya'akob*, that the first steps toward reconciling with his brother Esau and being whole were taken.

As Jacob lay there totally alone, and as thoughts about his life passed through his mind, he had a vision—perhaps of an angel, perhaps of a man—who suddenly attacked him. The two wrestled in the mud on the shore. Through the night Jacob struggled to hold his own against the shadowy figure, but he could not grasp who or what the shadow was as they rolled about and grasped each other's limbs:

Who are you? What is your name? Are you an angel of God sent to test me? If you are sent by God, I know I cannot defeat you. I can only pray that you will have mercy upon me and become my protector. You clearly have a human form. Are you my brother, Esau? Did you ford the Jabbok under cover of darkness to attack me when I am most vulnerable? You carry the smells of a shepherd, and the skins you wear are clearly taken from your flocks. I know the smells and the skins, since I, too, have shepherded flocks. If we are so much alike, can we not transform this stranglehold into one of embrace and live together as brothers?

But what if you are not Esau? Pray, tell me your name? The dawn is breaking and you will surely be discovered. No longer will you be able to hide your identity in the shadows of the night. I will not let you go until you reveal to me who you are. Are you merely a figure of my imagination? Have I created you? Are you a part of me? Tell me!

sent his family...
Genesis 32:23–24.

a man...
The identification of the man as an angel is based on Hosea 12:4–5.

Who are you?...
Loosely based on Genesis 32:27–30.

shepherded flocks...
Based on Bereshit Rabbah 77:1–3.

As Jacob wrestled through the night with the strange presence, he was conscious of all the different forces in his life with which he struggled: God, Esau, the side of himself that haunted him like a shadow. He was surely confronting both the human and divine in his life—and he survived the confrontation. That night, all the parts of Jacob and all the parts of his life came together, and he would never be the same.

human and divine...
Genesis 32:29.

At sunrise, Jacob limped away from the shore of the Jabbok, having been wounded in his struggle.[17] This made him even more vulnerable to an attack from Esau. Yet, his night struggle had girded him to meet his brother, for he was no longer the Jacob who had tricked Esau and had been manipulated by Laban. Rather, by wrestling with the faceless stranger, he had come to grips with the forces within him and was ready to assume his identity as the progenitor of the people of Israel. Now that he finally acknowledged what his life had been up to this point, now that he knew who the real Jacob was, he was ready to assume his new identity as Israel, his name having been changed by the mysterious presence with whom he had wrestled.[18]

name having been changed...
Genesis 32:29.

Reconciling with Esau: Giving Back the Blessing

It was a changed Jacob who saw his brother approaching. Although Esau came with four hundred men, and Jacob should have feared for his life, he uncharacteristically stepped out in front of his wives and children and exposed himself to greater danger.[19] But this new Jacob was ready to assume full responsibility for his family. He bowed low to the ground seven times as he drew near Esau. This made him even more vulnerable. A mature, wiser, and

stepped out in front...
Genesis 33:3.

more trusting Jacob understood that if he and Esau were ever to overcome their old struggle for position and power, then he had to find a way to propitiate his brother and give him the respect that he deserved, but which he had never received.

Esau ran...
Genesis 33:4.

Esau ran toward him and embraced him, and the two brothers wept. Jacob spoke to Esau, whom he had deceived and hurt years before:

to gain favor...
Based on
Genesis 33:8–11.

All that you see, all the animals, flocks, and possessions are meant only to gain favor in my Lord's eyes. I have not returned home harboring any thought of fighting with you. I do not come with an armed band of men ready to take up fight.[20] No, these are my wives, children, and servants who have come to pay you homage. Please accept this gift as a sign of my fidelity and of our relationship. All I want is to have you receive me favorably, to see me once again as your brother who desires only to please you and to return to you what is rightfully yours. God favored me during the years I dwelt in Laban's house. I have been blessed with plenty. I know that you, too, are a wealthy man and you don't need my gifts. But I need you to accept the gifts I have brought to you, anyway. I need to give back to you what I took from you many years ago. Please, take my blessing, I beseech you.[21]

As Esau heard Jacob's words and looked into his eyes he saw a different person from the one he remembered from twenty years before. The Jacob who limped toward him, embraced him, and pleaded with him to take back the blessing that he had stolen bore little resemblance to the conniver and trickster he had once known. Jacob had grown and matured. Now that he was middle-aged, he was able to ask forgiveness.[22]

Witnessing a transformed Jacob, a strong-willed person with integrity, Esau saw someone he liked and could easily identify with; someone more like himself. And without thinking at all, he suggested to Jacob that they travel together to Seir, which was Esau's home, to live together again in new-found harmony.

travel together...
Genesis 33:12–16.

But Jacob, to his credit, realized that though their moment of reconciliation had freed them from their youthful struggle for power, it would be better for both of them to live at some distance from each other. Though Esau had a romantic notion of a shared life together under the same roof, Jacob was mature enough to intuit that they needed to live apart from each other, since they were very different human beings. Even if they had been close all those years, they would have needed the space for their respective families to flourish.[23]

So as Esau started out on his journey toward Seir, thinking that Jacob would follow him, Jacob turned westward, eventually settling peacefully (*shalem*) in Shechem. Though he was limping after his confrontation at the Jabbok, he was anything but fragile. He was now whole—*shalem*—as he had never been before, not just because he had survived the encounter with Esau, who had threatened to kill him years before, but also because he had achieved a degree of wholeness in his person that was evident in all his actions.

Esau started out...
Genesis 33:15–18.

wholeness in his person...
Based on Targum Neophiti to Genesis 33:18.

Although Jacob did not settle near Esau, the two brothers maintained contact over the years, and both flourished in their own right. Jacob assumed the position of his father, Isaac. He settled in Canaan, the land promised by God to his ancestors, and he visited his aged father frequently, paying homage to him as he deserved. The last time he visited Isaac was at Kiryat Arba, Hebron, just before Isaac's death.[24]

He settled...
Genesis 33:18.

visited Isaac...
Genesis 35:27–29 and The Book of Jubilees 31:5–7.

But Jacob did not bury his father alone. He was joined by his brother Esau, who traveled from Seir in the southeast to bury Isaac in the Cave of Machpelah. The two brothers were united once more, and the years and the struggles between them vanished as they laid their father to rest. As Jacob grew older the events of the past began to fade, and he came to understand what he shared with Esau: their family history and the affection they both had felt for their father. He focused upon that as he built his future.

The Struggle Between Jacob and Israel

He settled...
Genesis 34:18–19.

Jacob came back to Canaan radically different from the person who had fled to Haran over twenty years before. He settled in Shechem with a new sense of peace in his life, and set up an altar there to the God of Abraham and Isaac, who had ensured his survival during his years in exile.

Reflecting back on that time in his life, Jacob remembered how fulfilled and happy he had been. He had everything for which to be grateful, and all he looked forward to in those days was seeing his family flourish and his sons assuming leadership of their people. Little did he realize then what was in store for him and just how difficult those years would be, as his children matured and came into their own. As much as he had changed during his years in Laban's house and when he confronted his brother near the Jabbok River, he hadn't understood or anticipated that his struggle would continue. If only he had known then what he knew now, as he prepared to bestow blessings on his own grandchildren, about the difficulty of transferring the mantle of leadership to the next generation. How could he have ever anticipated what would happen to his family after they had purchased land from the people of Shechem and settled there?

Shortly after they arrived, Jacob's only daughter, Dinah, was taken by force and raped by Shechem, the son of

Hamor. Upon hearing that his daughter had been defiled, Jacob kept silent, perhaps hoping unconsciously that everyone would forget about what had happened.

Upon hearing...
Genesis 34:1–5.

> Dear God, why have you allowed this thing to happen to me and my family? Why now, just when we have settled in this land and begun to put down roots and build for the future? What should I do? How can I possibly go out and confront Hamor and his people? Not only do they far outnumber us, but we are newly arrived here and seek to live in peace. Perhaps it isn't as serious as they are saying. Maybe Dinah likes this fellow Shechem, and it all can be worked out. I shouldn't overreact. It will be okay. But what should I do?

But what had occurred could not be ignored. And when Shechem's father, Hamor, confronted Jacob, asking for Dinah's hand in marriage for his son, Jacob's sons reacted vehemently. This was in marked contrast to their father's quiescence. Feigning agreement, they said that the men of Shechem must circumcise themselves, and on this condition they would give their daughters in marriage. While the Shechemites were recuperating from their circumcisions, Simon and Levi attacked the city of Shechem, killed all the males, took Dinah from Shechem's house, and returned her to her people.

Hamor, confronted...
Genesis 34:6–29.

Jacob, who had survived the encounter at the Jabbok and the confrontation with Esau, had little influence on his own children. Perhaps he didn't even raise a strong voice against what they planned to do. Surely this Jacob, the mature Jacob who had outfoxed Laban and knew how to deal effectively with a brother who had threatened to kill him, should have seen what would happen. The truth was that his sons did not care how their father might react and did not even take counsel with him. But it was worse. After Simon and Levi murdered the Shechemites, Jacob castigated his sons, but not with great vigor or conviction:

did not even take counsel...
Bereshit
Rabbah 80:10.

How could you do this to me? To our people? You have brought trouble upon all of us, making us odious among the inhabitants of this land. We have just returned to the place of our ancestors, hoping to reclaim what was promised to my fathers, Abraham and Isaac. Now our life here is threatened. We are so few in number that if all the peoples of Canaan hear what we have done to the people of Shechem and think that we cannot be trusted to live among them, we shall be destroyed if they unite against us. You have ruined everything!

While criticizing his sons, Jacob did not mention their brutality. He showed no concern or remorse over the death of innocent people. All that he could focus upon was his own reputation. How could he view the killing of so many people as having brought trouble upon *him*? Jacob seemed to have regressed. He was now concerned only with himself and his own welfare, and could not be a positive model for his own children. He had very little to say, and when he did speak, he seemed absorbed with himself. Perhaps as he approached the later stages of his life he no longer controlled events surrounding him; instead, he was controlled by them.[25]

Jacob's regression was most evident in God's concern about the name by which Jacob would be called. Following the events in Shechem, God seemed to need to remind him that his name had been changed as a result of the confrontation with the stranger at the Jabbok:

You shall be called...
Based on
Genesis 35:10.

You shall be called Jacob no more. Your name has been changed to Israel as a result of your struggle on your journey back to this land. Why do you still call yourself Jacob? You are now Israel, having assumed the responsibility for your people and their future. You don't seem to fully understand this. How long will that take? Will you ever be able to truly embrace the essence of your being and live up to the challenge that being the heir of Abraham and Isaac places upon you?

Jacob's withdrawal into himself and his subsequent inability to deal with his children were exacerbated by the painful loss of his beloved Rachel. When Rachel died in childbirth near the city of Ephrath, a part of Jacob died as well. In suddenly losing the love of his life, Jacob saw himself as even more of a victim, as someone who could no longer command the respect of his people.

Rachel died...
Genesis 35:16–18.

This was immediately evident when, after Rachel's death, Reuven, his firstborn son and the eldest child of Leah, went and slept with Bilhah, his father's concubine. By doing this, he also blasphemed Rachel's memory in his father's eyes, because he lay with her handmaid. Reuven seemed to be declaring that he was ready to displace his father and claim his birthright as the firstborn.

Reuven...
Genesis 35:22.

How did Jacob respond to this usurpation of his power and rights? He said absolutely nothing. His silence was as noticeable on this occasion as it had been during his sons' attack on the men of Shechem. Jacob's passivity was contributing to the unraveling of his family, and he could not see it. He only wanted his family to remain together, but it was about to break apart.[26]

Joseph: Jacob's Last Hope

As Jacob lay waiting in his tent for Joseph and his two sons, ruminating about his life, he understood that Joseph had become the focus of almost all of his attention and energy. He realized that he saw Joseph as his heir and that he saw himself in Joseph.[27]

he saw...
Bereshit
Rabbah 84:8.

As Rachel's firstborn son, Joseph had become, to Jacob, the incarnation of her in his life. He loved Joseph more than he loved his other children, and he constantly doted

He loved...
Genesis 37:3.

upon him as one would dote upon a grandchild. He set him apart from all his brothers by giving him the ornamented tunic worn by Leah and Rachel on their respective wedding nights, which was originally intended for Reuven, since he was Jacob's firstborn son.[28] As Jacob placed the tunic, also known as "the coat of many colors," on Joseph's shoulders, the boy felt the power that was now his. When his brothers saw how their father treated Joseph, they grew very jealous, and he, in turn, lorded over his brothers even more. The result was that all of Jacob's other sons hated Joseph, and he became totally alienated from them.

Jacob noticed his sons' jealousy, even their hatred, of Joseph, but he felt powerless to do anything. He simply kept his feelings to himself, never uttering a word of condemnation and never interceding. It seemed to Jacob that it was too late for that.

kept his feelings...
Genesis 37:11.

What am I to do? Joseph is caught up in his visions of grandeur and his haughty behavior. He acts as if he really believes his dreams in which his brothers and I bow down to him and worship him. He is totally oblivious to the impact his ridiculous dreams and obnoxious behavior have on his brothers; he is oblivious to the fact that all of them are aligned against him. I wish I could make them see how they treat each other, but it's too late. Even the sons of Bilhah and Zilpah hate him. His arrogance has united all my other sons against him. If only I had intervened earlier, when they were younger and we saw the first signs of the rivalry. Besides, perhaps it was my fault that things have turned out this way.

If I had not doted upon him so much, if I had not made it so obvious that he was my favorite, things might have been different. But I couldn't help myself. Every time I look at him, I see his mother Rachel. But there must be some way to overcome the jealousy, some way to bring my sons together. If only there were an opportunity for them to spend time together away from this house, away from me and from how they view my treatment of them.

So when the brothers went northward to find better grazing for the sheep, Jacob seized the opportunity to try to reconcile Joseph and his hostile siblings. For all his passivity, Jacob still felt obliged to try to guide his sons. He thought that if only they could spend time together, they would eventually see one another differently. Perhaps his motive was shaped by his own life experiences vis-à-vis his own brother. Just as he had had to confront Esau upon his return from Paddan-aram, so, too, Joseph would have to venture from home in order to confront his brothers on his own. In effect, Jacob was sending him into Esau's arms, with the hope that the brothers would embrace Joseph as Esau had embraced him by the Jabbok.[29] By this act, perhaps Joseph would grow and mature, and the family could be brought together again. Little did Jacob realize what would happen when Joseph found his brothers camped in Dothan. He could not have anticipated the pain and anguish that awaited him.

brothers went...
Genesis 37:12ff.

CHAPTER EIGHT

THE OLDER JACOB

Old Age

Erik Erikson: Stage Eight
Ego Identity vs. Despair

- Strength is experienced in old age as the accumulation of knowledge and wisdom over a lifetime, as well as a realization of the relativity of one's knowledge. This leads to mature judgment. It is also a time to expand one's concerns: The whole world becomes significant to the older person.

- This is time for life review—being aware of past experiences and the ability to confront unresolved problems. Individuals are ready to put their lives in order and to hand over their legacy to others, and to feel and think through what they will leave to the next generation.

- In old age, one finds meaning in life by accepting what life has meted out, and also by accepting imminent death and adapting to life's disappointments as well as its triumphs. Ego-integrity fosters a sense of wholeness at the end of one's life.

- The dangers of focusing on the self and assessing the full scope of one's life are ego-preoccupation, self-gratification, and disengagement from life and from people. Also, the feeling that life is too short can lead to despair and the fear of death.

It seemed that Jacob had waited a very long time for Joseph to bring his two sons, Ephraim and Manasseh, for blessing. Perhaps Jacob had been waiting for this moment ever since Rachel's death on the road near Ephrath. While waiting to see his grandchildren for the first time, Jacob couldn't help but think about the fact that their grandmother was not alive to enjoy them:

ever since Rachel's death...
See the connection between the blessing of Joseph's sons and Rachel's death in Genesis 48:7.

My life has not been the same since the day my beloved Rachel died giving birth to Benjamin as we sojourned in the land of Canaan in search of a place to settle permanently. Her labor had been very difficult. The months that she carried our son seemed endless; she was in constant pain and needed to be cared for frequently. But I never believed that she would not be able to survive the birth. When the midwife came out of the tent, all I had to do was look at her face to know that something dreadful had happened. My first thought was that the child had not survived. I would not allow myself to countenance the idea that something had happened to Rachel.

When she first announced that it was a boy, I relaxed. Rachel was safe. She had survived the ordeal. But then it became clear. The child was indeed alive, the one whom Rachel with her final breath called Ben Oni, the son of my affliction. But his mother, the person I loved most in this world, died that day.

his mother... died....
Based loosely on Genesis 35:16–19.

At first, I tried to see the child as an extension of Rachel, a sign that she was still alive for me, still a part of my life. I did not want my son to have to carry the name Rachel had given him. I could not bear seeing him as a constant reminder of the pain that she bore during his birth, and of the tragedy of her loss. And so I called him Benjamin, the son of my strength, my right hand.

Benjamin...
Genesis 35:18.

But no matter how hard I try, I cannot stop missing her. I still feel totally bereft and alone. The person with whom I shared my deepest feelings is no longer with me. There is nothing left for me. When she died on the road to Ephrath, all my energy was drained. In a way, I, too, died that day. Rachel's death was my death.[1] Since that day, my grief has been interminable. Her death was my greatest misfortune. It altered my entire life.

my greatest misfortune...
Bereshit Rabbah 97 (MSV).

Jacob wanted to harbor only fond memories of Rachel, to remember her as she was when he had first laid eyes on her at the well. Yet, God would not have it that way. Her tragic death at such a young age left Jacob with a vision of a Rachel consumed by pain, gasping her final breath with the knowledge that she would never live to see Benjamin grow and mature. For Rachel, the newborn would forever be her *Ben Oni*, the son of her affliction.

Jacob Withdraws Totally

If Rachel's death had a drastic effect upon Jacob, depriving him of love and companionship, the loss of his favored son, Joseph, made his life almost unbearable. He would live out the remainder of his days in mourning, refusing to be comforted. Better that his soul would descend to Sheol, the netherworld, to join his beloved Joseph, who surely was dead.

in mourning...
Genesis 37:34–35.

From the moment he was shown the tunic he had given Joseph, which was now dripping with blood, Jacob had withdrawn further and further into himself. His silence was palpable. He rarely spoke and never involved himself in his sons' affairs. He led a solitary, insular life, cutting himself off from his sons, his family, and the world.[2]

The only thing that kept Jacob alive was his only remaining link to Rachel—Benjamin. In Joseph's absence, simply seeing Benjamin and being near him was comforting. If he were to lose this son, there would no longer be any reason to go on living. Little did he know that sending his sons to Egypt to procure grain during the bitter famine that spread over the entire land would lead to more pain. Upon returning to Canaan, the sons told Jacob that the Pharaoh's viceroy had accused them of spying and that Simon was being held until they returned home and brought Benjamin with them. Having lost Joseph, Jacob now contemplated the fate of Benjamin and the loss of Rachel's second child as he spoke to his sons:

Why is this happening...
Based on
Genesis 42:36–38.

Why is this happening to me? It is always me whom you bereave. Joseph is no more, Simon has not returned from Egypt, and now you want to take Benjamin away from me. These things always happen to me! No, I won't listen. Don't make any promises. I don't believe any of you. You will not return Benjamin safely to me. I shall lose him forever. I tell you this: My son must not go to Egypt with you. His brother is dead, and Benjamin is all that I have. I will be left alone. If he meets with disaster on the journey, you will send my white head down to Sheol in grief. No! I will not permit it.

And then he thought to himself:

I pray...
Genesis 43:13–14.

But do I really have a choice? I must let them take the boy back to Egypt, or else Simon will surely die. What can I do? I pray that El Shaddai will dispose the man with mercy toward my sons, that he may release to them their brother Simon, as well as Benjamin. If anything should happen to him, I will hold each of them accountable, especially Judah, who has personally guaranteed Benjamin's safety. But as for me—alas, I am bereaved and will continue to be so. I have now been forced to part with all that is precious to me in my entire life.

Hope in Egypt: Unification of the Family

Egypt represented for Jacob the despair and pain for which he and his family were apparently destined. After their long journey, which had begun so many years before with Abraham's departure from Haran, they now were subject to the constraints of exile.[3] Their descent to Egypt had ruptured the unity of his family and taken them away from the land that had been promised to them by God. A calamity had surely befallen them.

Yet, Jacob did not know that when he sent his sons to Egypt to search for grain, he had sent them on a journey that would lead them to Joseph and the reunion of their family. There was great hope for their family in Egypt, even though it had not been apparent when Jacob sent them there for rations at the outbreak of the famine.[4]

The brothers' sojourn in Egypt would ensure their survival as a family. Joseph would provide for their sustenance during the continuing years of famine, while the discovery that he was alive and their family had been reunited would buoy their father's spirits and give him new life. Jacob would again have something to live for: to see Joseph one more time before he died.

Joseph would provide...
Genesis 45:10ff.

When his sons returned from Egypt and told him the news about Joseph, his heart went numb. Could it be true? Could Joseph be alive in Egypt after all this time?

I hear all these stories of what has happened to him and how he has risen to the office of Viceroy of Egypt. But it still doesn't seem possible, after all this time. To think that Joseph survived being brought to Egypt by a band of Ishmaelites and sold into slavery. Enough! All I know is that my son Joseph, the apple of my eye, is alive, and I must see his face before I

Joseph...is alive...
Genesis 45:26–28.

die. But how can I even think about traveling to Egypt? It is such a long journey, and I am so frail. I will never survive. Please God, please be with me as You were with my grandfather Abraham when he went down to Egypt to escape the ravages of famine, as I do now.

The God of Jacob's fathers...
Genesis 46:2–4.

The God of Jacob's fathers responded to his pleas, assuring him that he would not be alone on his journey to Egypt. The Divine would be with him and would make his descendants into a great nation while they sojourned there. But God also promised Jacob that his descendants would return to the land given to their ancestors. The fulfillment of God's past promises was guaranteed, while Jacob's happiness would be assured by being reunited with his beloved son, Joseph. Joseph would be his comfort in the final days of his life, and he would be at his side to close his eyes at the moment of his departure from this life.

So Jacob again journeyed from the Promised Land, this time with his entire family: his children and grandchildren and his entire clan. When Joseph heard that they had arrived in Goshen, out of sheer excitement at the prospect of seeing his father, he himself prepared his chariot so he could go out and greet him.[5] When he saw his father, he ran toward him, falling on his neck and kissing him incessantly. Jacob, in turn, could not hold in his emotions:

he himself prepared...
Genesis 46:29.

> My son, my son. Who would ever have thought that I would live to see your face again? I can't believe my eyes; they must deceive me. Is it really you? Are you Joseph, the son of my old age? Or are you an illusion? Yes, your clothes are different, but I could never forget your face! Over these past few years, I have tried to remember your features. Yes, you have your mother's eyes. And yes, that is your smile. And that is the color of your skin. All these years, I felt that if I could just recall how you look, I would somehow keep you alive.

And now that you are indeed alive, now that I see you and hold you, my life is complete. I thank our God in heaven Who has kept me alive until this time, so that I could see your face. Now I can die, happy and satisfied, knowing that you live.

Now I can die...
Genesis 46:30.

Now, as Jacob lay waiting for Joseph to bring Ephraim and Manasseh, he thought:

How ironic that the family is finally together again and that this has happened in Egypt, of all places. For as long as I can remember, there has always been strife among us. I can't think of a time when we lived together in harmony, when there was peace among all my sons. And now, far from the land of our ancestors, from the place that God promised to Abraham and Isaac, now we are together as one.

Despair Overtakes Jacob

Despite his elation, Jacob's life was a constant struggle. He always seemed to vacillate between feelings of achievement and satisfaction on one hand, and isolation and weakness on the other. When you live with inner conflict all your life, it is impossible to escape feelings of despair, even as you near death. So even though Jacob was elated to see Joseph and felt that his life was now complete, when he was presented to Pharoah by his son, he instinctively revealed his inner torment. Pharoah innocently asked him how many years he had lived, but Jacob bared his soul to him as he reflected on his life:[6]

Pharoah innocently asked...
Genesis 47:7–9.

My hundred and thirty years have been full of hardship. Few have been the times of real joy and satisfaction for me. When I look back on my life, all I can see is pain, deception, servitude, familial strife, famine, bereavement—and now exile from my homeland. I have frequently prayed to the God of

My hundred and thirty years...
Based on
Genesis 47:9.

my fathers to take my life and end my sojourn here on earth, since I have lived most of my days mourning lost dreams and bemoaning my fate. What will they say about me when I am gone? How will they compare me with my grandfather and father?[7] I will not have lived as long as they did, and I will not die content and fulfilled as they did.[8] I pray for God to release me from this torment.

Jacob's inner pain and torment became so severe that it affected him physically. Though up to this point he had not experienced any kind of disability in his life, save for the injury he had sustained in the struggle by the Jabbok, he suddenly became ill. It seemed as if he could no longer bear the tragedies that life had heaped upon him.

fell ill...
Genesis 48:1.

His entire family was stunned when Jacob fell ill. Jacob's father, Isaac, had never been sick before his death, and Abraham had never suffered before he died.[9] Jacob had frequently indicated that he felt his days were numbered, yet nothing ever happened to him. Only a few months before, Jacob had summoned Joseph to him,

his son swear...
Genesis 47:29–31.

telling him that he would soon die, and he made his son swear that he would carry his remains back to Canaan and bury him in the Cave of Machpelah. But once again, much time passed and Jacob remained in good health. So when Joseph received word that his father was deathly ill, he rushed to his bedside.

Anticipating Jacob's Death: A Chance for Closure

Though Jacob's illness came as a shock to the entire family, it did give them time to accustom themselves to his impending death and also to heal past wounds and ensure their bonding together. A parent's sudden death often pre-

prevents the settling...
Bereshit Rabbah 97
(MSV).

vents the settling of affairs with his or her children, but

Jacob was now given an opportunity to bring wholeness to his life and to his children's lives.

Though Jacob was in great pain, he lay in his tent eagerly anticipating the arrival of Ephraim and Manasseh with Joseph for his blessing. He had lived a long life, and, for all his suffering, he knew that God had blessed him. When his sons had brought him Joseph's coat covered with blood, he had thought that his beloved Joseph had been killed. He never expected to see Joseph again. Now, almost miraculously, he could bless Joseph's children, making them his own by placing them upon his knees as a sign of formal adoption.

see Joseph again...
Genesis 48:11.

Joseph, God blessed me at the outset of my life's journey, promising to make my descendants numerous and prosperous and to give them the land of Canaan as an everlasting possession. Now, even though I find myself in this strange land, I have been blessed by seeing you again and laying my eyes on your children. Your two sons, Ephraim and Manasseh, who were born to you here in this land of strangers before I came to you, shall be my sons no less than Reuven and Simon.[10] I do this not only as a way of showing how God has fulfilled the divine promise, but also out of respect for the memory of your mother, whom I loved dearly. I have lived for many years with the burden of her loss, recalling daily her death on the road to Ephrath.[11] Now, with the birth of your two sons, her memory will surely live on. Her grandchildren, your sons, are therefore as dear to me as my own children. Ephraim and Manasseh are a part of God's promise to me; they will inherit portions of the land equal to those of all of my sons.

Joseph, God blessed...
Based on Genesis 48:3–7.

Preparing to bless Ephraim and Manasseh, Jacob thought about his own life and his relationship with his own father, Isaac, and his brother, Esau, and the blessings

**embraced and
kissed...**
Genesis 48:10.

they had received. At that moment, he instinctively
reached out and embraced and kissed his grandchildren,
touching them in a way that his own father never touched
him. Though he had been blessed by Isaac, he had never
felt his father's warmth and love, which perhaps had been
reserved for Esau. What good was the blessing without a
parent's love? He had often thought of the moment when
his father blessed him, and these reflections were always
full of pain and estrangement. He knew his father had not
loved him as much as his brother.

Now, as Jacob stood in front of his two grandchildren he
was flooded with emotions of past triumph and rejection.
Here, finally, was an opportunity to undo the past, to overcome the very conflict that had shaped his entire life. He
had a chance to give each grandchild an appropriate blessing, although he was blessing them at the same time.

father stretched...
Genesis 48:14ff.

Joseph was astonished when his father stretched forth his
right hand and placed it upon Ephraim's head, though he
was the younger, while putting his left hand on Manasseh.
Joseph objected strenuously as his father crossed his
hands—in order, it seemed, to give Ephraim the blessing
of the firstborn.[12] Joseph thought that his father wanted to
perpetuate the same sibling rivalry from which he had suffered. But when Joseph attempted to switch Jacob's hands,
Jacob assured his son that both children were to be
blessed:

Joseph, Joseph...
Based on Genesis
48:15–16 and 19–20.

Joseph, Joseph, it is all right. Do not fear. Though I know that
you want Manasseh as the firstborn to be given preference, it
cannot be that way. His children will surely become a great
tribe, but not as numerous as his younger brother's progeny.
Yet, both of these children shall be blessed, and neither is
more preferred in God's eyes.[13] Both will be part of our
covenanted people; both shall inherit portions on the
Promised Land. Both shall be called by my name.

And now…Ehpraim and Manasseh, by you every child in Israel shall be blessed. Your blessing shall be theirs. Every parent shall bless his or her children by saying, "God shall make you like Ephraim and Manasseh."

May the God who has been my shepherd from the day of my birth to this day, the Angel who redeemed me from all harm, bless these children. Through them, my name shall be recalled, as well as the names of my grandfather Abraham and my father Isaac, and may they become teeming multitudes upon the earth.

Although Jacob was about to die, he finally felt that the future of his family was guaranteed. God, Who had promised the constant presence of the Divine in their lives, would be with them throughout their sojourn in Egypt, thus ensuring their return to the land of their ancestors. Another guarantee that they would return to the land of Canaan was that Jacob had made Joseph swear to bury him there. God also comforted Jacob by saying that when he died, Joseph would be there to close his eyes. The family was together again in perpetuity, and their people's presence on their ancestral land was ensured. Jacob was now ready to die, knowing that his family—and he—had come to wholeness.

God…would be with them… Based mainly on

Blessing His Sons: Viewing the Future

As death rapidly approached, Jacob readied himself for the inevitable. Accepting the fact that God was about to take him, he tended to the important tasks at hand: to bless his children as he had been blessed, to make arrangements for his burial, and to make sure that the mantle of leadership was passed to the next generation.[14]

Unlike his father and grandfather, in the final moments of his life Jacob gained a clarity of vision that gave him a new perspective on his life and that of his people. Past, present, and future were arrayed before his very eyes, and he saw with great precision how their future would fulfill the promises made to his father and grandfather. Though far from their homeland, Jacob knew that his progeny would live in the land of Canaan in covenant with their God, and he was impelled to communicate these hopes to them. For all that he had failed to do as a father, he finally succeeded in his most important task: articulating to his sons who they were and the role that each of them would play in the ongoing saga of their people.[15] Through this, Jacob provided them with a strong sense of family identity and destiny.

Jacob called...
Genesis 49:1.

Having blessed Joseph's sons, Ephraim and Manasseh, Jacob called all his sons together so he could share with each of them what would happen to them in the days to come. Unlike his forebearers, he included all his sons in his final blessings. To be sure, each of his sons was different and each deserved a distinctive blessing, but none would be left out. All would have a share in the blessing that had been given originally to Abraham and transmitted through Isaac. They were one people, one nation, and through their unity they would not only survive but flourish.[16] Unity was the most important condition for Israel's redemption.

Come, my sons...
Based on Genesis
49:1–2.

do you affirm...
Bereshit Rabbah
98:3–4 and B.T.
Pesahim 56a.

Come, my sons, gather together so that I may speak to all of you about your future and the future of our people. Gather, and listen, you sons of Jacob; listen to Israel, your father.[17] You who are called Israel, do you affirm that the God of our fathers, Abraham and Isaac, is your God? Is there anything in your hearts that would lead you to deviate from the belief of those who came before us? Do you accept the responsibilities of being God's covenanted people, to living lives of holiness dedicated to fulfilling the blessings that have been given to us?

And Jacob's sons responded to him, "Hear O Israel, our father, the Lord is our God, the Lord is One.[18] We pledge to continue affirming God's presence and unity through all that we do." On his deathbed, Jacob sought assurance that the values and beliefs he had inherited from Abraham and Isaac would be carried on for generations to come.[19] At the end of his life, just as every person struggles with his or her own mortality, Jacob needed to gain a sense that his life would continue through his children. When he finally heard that they had internalized his values and beliefs, and that they were indeed the people of Israel, he knew that who he was and what he stood for would live on after him.[20] Past, present, and future merged for Jacob in this moment, and his life was crowned with hope.[21]

Aware of the importance and meaning of his family's history, Jacob portrayed his progeny's future as a continuation of their covenantal relationship with God and as movement toward their ultimate destiny.[22] Although his life had been fraught with deep disappointments, he knew that greatness awaited his children as he saw their lives arrayed before him. Although they were about to suffer during their sojourn in Egypt, they would experience harmony and fulfillment. That was the end toward which Jacob pointed his descendants: Their eventual destiny was to live as one people united with their God on the land promised to their ancestors.[23]

Jacob experienced great despair near the end of his life; he had suffered painful losses and traumatic conflicts within his family. Yet, he drew upon his own spiritual resources as he blessed each of his sons. Although Jacob recognized that the nation's future would be built through the tribes of

deep disappointments... Some of them are alluded to in his blessings of Reuven, Simon, and Levi in Genesis 49:3–5.

Judah and Joseph, the descendants of each of his sons would also have an important share in their common destiny. So Jacob blessed each son, characterizing the future of each, and basing it in part upon each of their pasts. To his credit—and reflecting his insight as a parent—he recognized their individuality and tailored his blessings to each son's uniqueness.

tailored his blessings...
Genesis 49:28.

Though perhaps it came a bit late in his life, Jacob's strength of character was also evident in his blessings. In condemning the disgraceful and violent acts of Reuven, Simon, and Levi, he challenged all of his future progeny—and the entire Jewish nation—about the values by which they would live. If the people of Israel were to survive and fulfill their destiny, then they had to continue to grow and mature. They, like their father Jacob, would have to struggle with their higher selves until they could become Israel.[24]

Jacob's Release—and His Redemption

redemptive presence...
This wish is interjected into the sequence of his blessings in Genesis 49:18.

I am about to be gathered...
Based on Genesis 49:29–50:5.

I cannot depart...
Based loosely on Genesis 50:16–17.

Jacob had suffered in many ways, but his last moments were filled with the hope of experiencing a sense of wholeness that he had never had during his entire life. He longed for that very feeling of God's redemptive presence as he blessed each of his sons:

My sons, I am about to be gathered to my kin. I have only two requests of you. First, I cannot depart from you knowing that you still harbor evil thoughts about one another. I implore you to forgive one another. What you did to Joseph was harsh and inhuman. He is your brother, and you must ask his forgiveness. You, Joseph, must understand that you are a part of this family, one of twelve great tribes that will one day flourish on our land. No matter how much power you now possess, your life is intertwined with that of your brothers, and the future of our people will be shaped by their descendants as much as yours.

Promise me, my children, that you will put the past to rest and build together for our future. Tell me that you will love one another and cherish the ties that bind our family as one—one people covenanted with the God Who created heaven and earth.

Finally, I want to be buried with our ancestors in the Cave of Machpelah, which is in the field that my grandfather Abraham purchased from Ephron, the Hittite. I prepared the grave myself, knowing that I would soon come to my end on this earth. Carry me back to the land of my fathers, to the land of Canaan, and lay me to rest in the Cave of Machpelah, which faces Mamre. Let me lie forever with those who came before us, so that future generations will know that our people must never again leave their homeland.

May you ever remember whence you have come, and that all of your ancestors, beginning with Adam and Eve almost twenty-five generations ago, stand with you as you look to the future.[25] May you be worthy of the gift that you have inherited.

When Jacob finished his instructions to his sons, he drew his feet into his bed, and with his last breaths, he was gathered to his people.

The Life of Joseph:
The Journey of the Jewish People

When he realized that his father was dead, Joseph flung himself upon Jacob and wept uncontrollably. His tears fell on his father's face as he kissed and stroked him. Sitting on Jacob's deathbed, he could not help but feel grateful that he had had the opportunity to bring Ephraim and Manasseh to his father for a blessing.

Joseph flung...
Genesis 50:1.

He was sure that his father also felt that this was a crowning moment in his own life. Jacob had finally seen his family come together, and now his grandsons were the symbols of their people's past and future. He had succeeded in doing what most of us dream of for our old age: preparing our children to assume responsibility for carrying on our family's values and traditions. And so, when Jacob blessed them, he recounted the journey of his family from its very inception, all the way back to Abraham.[1] Similarly, when Jacob blessed Joseph, he emphasized that all the blessings of the past would rest upon Joseph's head, since he was the heir to all that had preceded him.

blessings of the past...
Genesis 49:24–26.

As for Joseph, when Jacob placed his hands upon the heads of Ephraim and Manasseh, it was as if he, Joseph, were being blessed, because the future began with him.[2] Every child of Israel yet to be born would be blessed through his progeny. The blessing his father had given to him was also a sign of the future greatness of the people of Israel, all of whom would surely prosper on the land that was promised to Abraham, Isaac, and Jacob.

child of Israel...
Genesis 48:20.

surely prosper...
Genesis 50:24.

Joseph understood that his own life's journey anticipated the future journey of his people. He recognized early that a providential hand was guiding him. All that would befall him was God's doing, and his life would be associated with the destiny of the Jewish people. In effect, his fate would transcend his own personal story and would be part of the story of the people of Israel: moving from despair to hope, from aloneness to covenant, from exile to redemption.[3]

God's doing...
See, for example, Genesis 45:7.

The moment Joseph was born, Jacob had begun to think of returning home and fulfilling his destiny. Though he had dwelt in Laban's house for twenty years, when Rachel gave birth to Joseph, the idea of Jacob's progeny living on their ancestral land in covenant with God took prominence. Even when Joseph suffered in Egypt, his growth and development that came out of the hardships he had to overcome anticipated his progeny's birth as a unified people as a result of their ultimate redemption from slavery.[4] Just as God had been with him when his brothers threw him into the pit and when he languished in prison in Egypt, so, too, the Divine would be with his children's children while they were in Egypt and would bring them back to the land of their fathers and mothers.[5]

Rachel gave birth...
Genesis 30:25.

bring them back...
Genesis 48:21 and 50:25.
carried their father's remains...
Genesis 50:7ff.

When Jacob died, Joseph and his brothers carried their father's remains back to the land of Canaan for burial in the Cave of Machpelah, as Jacob had instructed them to do. This way, he would be buried with his grandparents, Abraham and Sarah, and his parents, Isaac and Rebekkah, and would be reunited with his wife, Leah. The irony, of course, was that immediately after the entire family traveled to Canaan to bury their father, they returned to Egypt after observing mourning for seven days. Although Joseph and all his brothers had returned to Canaan, they were destined to die in exile, far from the Promised Land. Now, for the first time in the family's history, no member of their clan dwelt in the land promised to their forebear. It seemed that Egypt would forever be their home.

However, even though Joseph would live to see the birth of great-grandchildren in Egypt, and even though he intuited that his family would suffer a protracted exile there, he always knew that God would eventually redeem them and return them to the land of the covenant.[6] And at the end of his life, he would recall God's promise that Canaan would be theirs:

live to see...
Genesis 50:23.

> My brothers, I am about to die and be gathered to our people. Though we no longer live on our land, and we probably will remain in exile for many years, God will eventually return us to the land that the Divine promised to our great-grandfather, Abraham, to our grandfather, Isaac, and to our beloved father, Jacob. Here in Egypt we have become a unified family, and our numbers have begun to increase. Though there are no guarantees that the favor we now enjoy from Pharoah and his leaders will continue, I know in my heart that our God will not abandon us. The future is one of great promise, and we will again enjoy life on our holy soil.
>
> Therefore, when the time comes for you or your descendants to return to the land of our ancestors, swear to me that you will carry my bones from here so that I, too, may dwell in our land. When our people's story is complete, may it be told that our time here in Egypt, a foreign land, was preparation for all that shall follow, for the fulfillment of the promise of our future greatness.

I am about to die...
based loosely on Genesis 50:24–25.

The story of Joseph and his brothers, the progeny of Abraham, Isaac, and Jacob, ends with Joseph's death and burial in Egypt. They do not carry him back to the land of Canaan; he and they remain in exile.[7] Yet, the promise of redemption is underscored by the pledge to take Joseph's bones back with them when they return to their land. In the moment of his death, Joseph becomes the symbol of his people's future.

In one sense, Joseph's life story represents the replaying of the entire journey of his people: its inception in Paddan-aram through the period of maturation in the land of Canaan until its immersion in Egypt. Joseph, too, developed over time from a pampered youth; to a frightened adolescent who was enslaved; to the viceroy of Egypt; to a family person who enjoyed his role as father, son, and brother; and finally to one who possessed a vision of his people's future.

Yet, his life also presaged the experiences of his descendants. Joseph succeeded in vanquishing the bitterness and hostility from which he had suffered, transforming them into love for his siblings within a closely knit family. Stripped of all his youthful illusions, he matured into a leader of his people and died quite contentedly in his old age. Through his journey from spoiled child to enslaved adolescent to powerful leader and, finally, to visionary at the end of his life, the contours of the path that his progeny would take had already been shaped.[8]

Erik Erikson's Psychological Developmental Levels*

Developmental Level	Basic Task	Negative Counterpart	Basic Virtues
1. Infant	Basic trust	Basic mistrust	Drive and hope
2. Toddler	Autonomy	Shame and doubt	Self-control and willpower
3. Preschooler	Initiative	Guilt	Direction and purpose
4. School-ager	Industry	Inferiority	Method and competence
5. Adolescent	Identity	Role confusion	Devotion and fidelity
6. Young adult	Intimacy	Isolation	Affiliation and love
7. Middleescent	Generativity	Stagnation	Production and care
8. Older adult	Ego-integrity	Despair	Renunciation and wisdom

*Taken from Clara Shaw Schuster and Shirley Smith Ashburn, *The Process of Human Development: A Holistic Approach* (Philadelphia: Lippincott–Raven, 1980), p. 914. Reprinted by permission of the publisher.

Introduction

1. Howard Cooper, "In the Beginning: Chaos, Creation and Theory," *European Judaism* 22 (Winter 1989): 3–4.
2. See, for example, Erik Erikson's "Eight Ages of Man," in his *Childhood and Society*, 2nd ed. (New York: W. W. Norton and Company, 1963), 247–274.
3. For a simple chart of Erikson's eight stages, see the Appendix, which is drawn from Clara Shaw Schuster and Shirley Smith Ashburn, *The Process of Human Development: A Holistic Approach* (Boston: Little, Brown and Co., 1980), 914.
4. Stephen Crites, "The Narrative Quality of Experience," *Journal of the American Academy of Religion* 39 (1981): 294.
5. Bill Buford, "Comment: The Seduction of Storytelling," *The New Yorker*, June 24, 1996, 12.
6. Crites, "The Narrative Quality," 304.
7. The term *midrash* is based on the verb *darash*, which means "seek," "search," or "demand." The process of *midrash* is to search out contemporary meaning from Scripture.
8. Wolfgang Iser, *The Act of Reading* (Baltimore: Johns Hopkins Press, 1978), 107.
9. Ibid., 157.
10. Aviva Zornberg, *Genesis: The Beginning of Desire* (Philadelphia: The Jewish Publication Society, 1995), xviii.
11. Barry Holtz, *Back to the Sources: Reading the Classic Jewish Texts* (New York: Summit, 1984), 29.
12. See Carol Ochs, *The Song of the Self: Biblical Spirituality and Human Holiness* (Valley Forge, Pa.: Trinity Press, 1994), 11–12 and 66, ff for allusions to this approach to the Book of Genesis.

Chapter One: Adam and Eve

1. See Elie Wiesel, *Messengers of God* (New York: Random House, 1976), 3, 12.
2. Arthur Waskow, in *Godwrestling* (New York: Schocken Books, 1978), 50, beautifully describes human life as a journey

between two gardens: the garden of our infancy and the garden of our maturity.

3. Naomi Rosenblatt and Joshua Horwitz, *Wrestling with Angels* (New York: Dell Publishing, 1995), 8.

4. These musings of Adam are based in part on Peter Pitzele, *Our Fathers' Wells* (San Francisco: HarperSanFrancisco, 1995), 18.

5. See Betsy Halpern Amaru, "The First Woman: Wives and Mothers in Jubilees," *Journal of Biblical Literature* 113 (1994): 609; and Joel Rosenberg, "The Garden Story Forward and Backward," *Prooftexts* 1 (1981): 7.

6. See the discussion of *tzeila* as meaning "side" and its implications in my book *Self, Struggle & Change: Family Conflict Stories in Genesis and Their Healing Insights for Our Lives* (Woodstock, Vt.: Jewish Lights Publishing, 1995), 26–27.

7. Genesis 2:16 reads: *Va-Y'tzav…'al Ha-Adam*, which literally means "[God] placed the command *on* Adam."

8. Rosenblatt and Horwitz, *Wrestling with Angels*, 31.

9. See, in this regard, Pitzele, *Our Fathers' Wells*, 30.

10. According to the tradition, the snake spoke in human language. See, for example, Philo, *On the Creation of the World*, in the Loeb Classical Library (Cambridge, Ma.: Harvard University Press, 1971), 56. The snake and Adam and Eve are also joined in a very direct way by a clear wordplay—the human beings are described as being *arumim*, "naked," while the snake is called *arum*, "shrewd." Interestingly, the word for snake in Aramaic is *hivia*, the same consonants that are found in Eve's name in Hebrew, *Hava*. It is not surprising then that the snake, like Satan, seems to represent the *Yetzer ha-Ra*, the Evil Inclination, in the eyes of the rabbis.

11. The snake is that voice in the human being which represents the impulse to challenge authority and the order of things as they are. As Peter Pitzele wrote in *Our Fathers' Wells*, 37, the serpent is the force that pushes us towards independence.

12. Rosenblatt and Horwitz, *Wrestling with Angels*, 36.

13. Michael Chernick, *Torah on Tapes* (Union of American Hebrew Congregations, 1990), Volume One, Side A.

14. Adam and Eve are described as being *arumim*, "naked," but the double entendre is clear: they possess no shame. They are naive, innocent. The intent is underscored when the snake is described as being *arum*, "clever" or "shrewd." He prods them into eating the fruit, and that causes them to lose their innocence and become aware of their sexuality.

15. Rosenblatt and Horwitz, *Wrestling with Angels*, 29.
16. Ochs, *The Song of the Self*, 7, 15. See also Zornberg, *Genesis: The Beginning of Desire*, 15.
17. Alicia Ostriker, *The Nakedness of the Fathers: Biblical Visions and Revisions* (New Brunswick, N.J.: Rutgers University Press, 1994), 21–22. Perhaps Adam and Eve had learned to play the game of hide-and-seek.
18. Adam claimed that they hid because they were naked, *arumim*. In a sense, they were naked, since they were "bare" of God's command. The Hebrew reads *eirom anochi* ("I am naked"), and the term *Anochi* is utilized more frequently with respect to God, especially as the first word in the Ten Commandments. For this play on *anochi*, see, for example, Mekhilta d'Rabbi Ishmael, *Massekhta d'Pisha, parashah* 5. But there is an additional play on words here, since the serpent is described as being *arum*, "shrewd." In a sense, Adam and Eve try to shrewdly evade God's presence, and they share much in common with the snake, who sheds his skin and also appears naked.
19. Michael Chernick points out that the word *mithalekh*, from the phrase "the sound of God was moving through the Garden" (Genesis 3:8), is a reflexive verb that could be understood as "God moving into the Divine self." It would, therefore, signify God's withdrawal in part from them. See Chernick's comments on *Torah on Tapes*, Volume One.
20. Since the snake is the only animal mentioned to have been in the Garden of Eden, it is possible that the garments made for Adam and Eve were woven from snake skins. How ironic! The very vehicle for their banishment and downfall, the snake, is the means by which they not only will survive outside the Garden but will grow and mature. In addition, the skin, in Hebrew *or* (which consists of the letters *ayin, vav, reish*), is part of a possible sound play with the word *or* (*aleph, vav, reish*), meaning "light." God's protective presence enveloped human beings on their journey in the "real" world outside the Garden.
21. Ostriker, *The Nakedness of the Fathers*, 35.
22. See, in this regard, the quotation from Dorothee Solle's book, *Great Women of the Bible in Art and Literature* in *Talking about Genesis: A Resource Guide*, eds. Christopher Leighton and Sandee Brawarsky (New York: Doubleday, 1996), 43, and Ochs, *The Song of the Self*, 83.

23. Pitzele, *Our Fathers' Wells*, 27. Pitzele so beautifully writes, "Eden before history becomes our model of Utopia at history's end."
24. See note 2 above.

Chapter Two: Cain and Abel

1. Devora Steinmetz, "Vineyard, Farm and Garden: The Drunkenness of Noah in the Context of Primeval History," *Journal of Biblical Literature* 113/2 (Summer 1994): 202.
2. Several classic *midrashim* contrast Cain and Abel in this regard, emphasizing that Abel refused to cultivate the land because he stood in awe of God. He thought that if the land had been cursed it would be sinful to work it. See, for example, Midrash Aggadah to Genesis 4:2 and Rashi's commentary to the same verse.
3. The classic conflict in folklore is between the farmer and the shepherd. Theirs is seen as a confrontation between opposing forces. Their conflict also reflects the Temple cult and its sacrificial system: animal sacrifices versus vegetable sacrifices. The text emphasizes the tension between the two when it says that "Abel became a keeper of sheep, but Cain became a tiller of the soil."
4. Yin and Yang in Chinese thought are perceived to be contrary, yet complementary, forces. The rabbis, too, emphasize the interdependency between Cain and Abel. See, in this regard, Pirkei d'Rabbi Eliezer, Chapter 21, and Midrash ha-Gadol to Genesis 4:2.
5. This is emphasized by the fact that in contrast, Abel's offering is described as "the firstlings [*bechorot*] of his flock." This, in effect, is "the choicest" (based on the play with the Hebrew word *bachar*). That is why Cain is compared to a bad tenant farmer who eats the ripe figs but presents the king with the late figs. See Bereshit Rabbah 22:5 in this regard.
6. The text implies that the sacrifices were Cain's idea. The text says: "And Abel also brought"—*Ve-Hevel hayvi gam hu*—which indicates that Abel saw the sacrifice Cain brought and followed suit. Abel learned what God expected from his brother.
7. The text never says that Cain sinned. All we are told is that God turned to, or paid attention to, Abel's sacrifice but did not pay attention to Cain's sacrifice. The Hebrew verb used is *sha'ah*, which literally means "to turn to." There is no implied rejection or even necessarily a value judgment. Perhaps it is all a matter of Cain's perception.

8. Ochs, *The Song of the Self*, 15.

9. Pitzele, *Our Fathers' Wells*, 55, 60.

10. Steinmetz, "Vineyard, Farm and Garden," 202.

11. God's statement can be understood either as a reference to the past, to what Cain had already done, or as a future address. God was saying either that Cain got what he deserved or that Cain had the power to make the best of his situation. The Hebrew verbs are in the future tense, *'im taitiv* ("if you will do right") and *timshol* ("you will control or master"), which probably should be read as a challenge to Cain and not as a past recollection. See, in this regard, Bereshit Rabbah 22:6.

12. Wiesel, *Messengers of God*, 63.

13. Rosenblatt and Horwitz, *Wrestling with Angels*, 56.

14. The time sequence of the scene in the Bible is not at all clear: "Cain said to his brother Abel...and when they were in the field, and Cain set upon Abel and killed him" (Genesis 4:8). We do not know if Cain went out to the field looking for his brother, or perhaps as we learn from the early translations of the Bible—such as the Septuaguint, the Peshitta, and some Aramaic Targumim—he asked Abel to take a walk in the fields with him.

15. Since Cain's words are missing from the biblical text, his intention when he spoke to his brother in Genesis 4:8 is not clear. Did he come to him with an angry accusation? Or was he seeking words of comfort?

16. Perhaps the ellipsis in the text is intentional. The biblical writer is communicating to the reader that Cain had every intention to speak to Abel. Indeed, he began to open his mouth, but there were literally no words.

17. Although the verse tells us that "Cain spoke to Abel," we never hear Abel's voice in the story. Abel is absolutely silent and totally passive. He is truly Abel, *Hevel* in Hebrew: "nothingness," a "wisp," a "shadow," "lacking all substance."

18. The play here is on the Hebrew word *sayt*, "uplift," from the root *nasa*.

19. For two very poignant descriptions of Cain's struggle with his primitive instincts, see Wiesel, *Messengers of God*, 39, and Pitzele, *My Fathers' Wells*, 55.

20. Based on the musical pointing (the *trop*) of the verse, almost all translations understand Cain's remark as "I do not know. Am I my brother's keeper?" However, in consonance with several *midrashim*, as Elie Wiesel pointed out in his *Messengers*

of God, 59, the text can be read without a break. This was Cain's defense: He was not aware of his responsibility.

21. The comment "You are the real murderer" is based on a creative play on the words *Ha-shomer 'achi Anochi* ("Am I my brother's keeper?"). The term *Anochi* ("I") can be understood as God's name, since it is used in relation to the Divine quite frequently, e.g., the first word of the Ten Commandments. Therefore, with a shift in the syntax, Cain's words could read, "*Anochi ha-shomer 'achi*," "God is my brother's keeper."

22. See Rosenblatt and Horwitz, *Wrestling with Angels*, 56.

23. In a *midrash* in Bereshit Rabbah 23:5, the rabbis emphasized that Cain himself was killed because he killed Abel. It was as if two trees were standing near each other in the forest. When a wind uprooted one of them, it fell upon the other and uprooted it as well.

24. See, in this regard, Gunther Plaut's comment on Genesis 4:9 in his *The Torah: A Modern Commentary* (New York: Union of American Hebrew Congregations, 1981), 47.

25. The phrase, "Am I [*Anochi*] my brother's keeper?" could be read as "Am I my brother's keeper, God?" if we take the word *Anochi* as a reference to the Divine and not simply to Cain.

26. Wiesel, *Messengers of God*, 42.

27. Most translations understand Cain's words in Genesis 4:13 to mean "My punishment [*avoni*] is too great to bear," even though the word *avon* usually means "sin." As the rabbis translate this passage ("My sin is too great to bear"), Cain is seen as a repentant sinner.

28. Cain's words are based on a passage in Devarim Rabbah 8:1. See Targum Yerushalmi to Genesis 4:10, Vayiqra Rabbah 10:5, Midrash Tanhuma ha-Nidpas Bereshit 9, and Midrash Lekah Tov to Genesis 4:10. It is also alluded to in Josephus' *Jewish Antiquities* 1:1.

29. Note the play on Micah's description of God as "the bearer of sin"—*nosei avon*—and Cain's words in Genesis 4:13: "My sin [*avoni*] is too great to bear [*mi-neso*]." There is also a distinct allusion to God's words in verse 7: "If you do right, there is uplift [*sayt*]," based on the same root. There can be no uplift for the human being without a recognition of the Other—i.e., God—in his or her life.

30. According to such *midrashim* as Bereshit Rabbah 22:13, the Pesiqta d'Rav Kahana 24:11, and Midrash ha-Gadol to Genesis 4:16, Cain was the model of repentance, having confessed before God.

31. Note the play between the phrase, "Cain rose up [*va-yakom*] against his brother, Abel" (Genesis 4:8) and "Seven-fold vengeance shall be taken on/come upon [*yukam*] anyone who kills Cain" (Genesis 4:15). The verbal play underscores the progression from Cain's killing Abel to God's protecting him. See Midrash Tadshe 20 in this regard, since it emphasizes that the name for God used throughout Genesis 4 is always *Adonai*, the symbol of God's compassion.

32. The word translated as "mark" in the Genesis 4:15 text is *ot*. This term is used to refer to two other things in the Book of Genesis: the rainbow after the Flood (Genesis 9:13), and circumcision, which is a "sign" of the covenant between God and the Jewish people (Genesis 17:11). The Sabbath is also referred to as an "eternal sign" of God's relationship with them.

33. Cain settles down, builds a family, and founds a city, which is named after his son, Enoch. He is pictured in Genesis 4:17–22 as the progenitor of civilization. See the comments by Steinmetz in "Vineyard, Farm and Garden," which suggest that Cain seems to internalize the consequences of his sin, thereby taking charge of his life. This stands in contrast to his father, Adam, following God's pronouncement of judgment upon him.

Chapter Three: Noah

1. Genesis 5:29 reads, "This one will provide us with relief [comfort] from our work and the toil [*itzavon*] of our hands, out of the very soil which *Adonai* placed under a curse." In providing an etymology for Noah's name, the biblical writer plays on the root *nacham* (comfort) and the name *Noach*. In so doing, he alludes in Genesis 3:7 to God's curse of the earth and the hardship [*itzavon*] of cultivating it.

2. In mentioning the hardship that humankind faced in tilling the soil, the biblical writer's point is clear: Noah would mollify God and make up for the sin in the Garden of Eden. In fact, when the text in Genesis 5:29 stresses that "This one [*zeh*] will provide us relief from our work [*mi-ma'aseinu*]," the term *ma'aseinu* could be interpreted to mean "our actions," alluding to the sin of Adam and Eve.

3. The text reads: "And the Lord regretted [*va-yenahem*] having made the human being on the earth, and the Divine's heart was saddened [*va-yitatzeiv al libo*]. Both Hebrew phrases allude to the explanation of Noah's name in the verse quoted

above, Genesis 5:29: "This one will provide us with relief
[*yenahameinu*]...from the toil [*me-itzavon*] of our hands."
Thus, the biblical writer helps us anticipate Noah's role in sav-
ing humanity and that he will bring comfort to God following
its sinfulness.

4. God notes a bit later in Genesis 8:21: "The devisings of the
human's heart are evil from his or her youth."

5. The phrase "primal degeneracy" is used by Peter Pitzele in his
poignant description of the Flood story in *Our Fathers' Wells*, 67.

6. Note the flow of the biblical comments in Genesis 6:7–8. God
says, "I regret [*nihamti*] that I made them," which is immediately followed by "*ve-Noah matzah hen*," which translates as
"but Noah found favor." The sound play between *naham* and
Noah matzah, which use the same Hebrew consonants, is
clear: Noah would be the antidote to God's anger and regret.

7. Genesis 6:9 literally reads: "These are the generations of
Noah; Noah was a blameless person in his age." The *midrash*
emphasizes that his legacy was not his progeny so much as his
actions. See, for example, Midrash Lekah Tov on this verse.
He begins to develop a sense of his own moral responsibility
over his peers. See also the comments of Aviva Zornberg in
Genesis: The Beginning of Desire, 68, in which she notes that,
in a sense, Noah was his own legacy, since the text reads:
"These are the generations of Noah; Noah..." He himself
developed into a primary moral agent. Only in the next verse
does the biblical writer tell us that Noah begat Shem, Ham,
and Yapheth.

8. Noah's devotion to the task and the fact that he took the initiative to fulfill all that God asked of him is evident in the text's
repetitious wording. Genesis 6:22 reads: "Noah did so; just as
God commanded him, so he did." The superfluous emphasis
on Noah's actions indicates his deep involvement in the task
at hand.

9. The text emphasizes twice that Noah carried out God's commands exactly as they were given. This is stated in Genesis
6:22 and again, almost word for word, in Genesis 7:5.

10. Noah's remarks are based upon a *midrash* in Tanhuma
Ha-Nidpas *Noah* 5.

11. In this regard, see Zornberg, *Genesis: The Beginning of
Desire*, 58.

12. The rabbis castigate Noah for his lack of concern for the rest
of humanity and for worrying only about himself. For example,
they contrast him with Abraham at the impending destruction

of Sodom and Gomorrah (Genesis 18) when he argues for the lives of the righteous. Noah never once challenges God's decree. Noah "walked *with* God" (Genesis 6:9), but Abraham, by contrast, walked *before* God (Genesis 17:1)—Abraham brought God to humanity. Noah was singled out for survival; Abraham for a mission. See, in this regard, Bereshit Rabbah 30:10, Yalqut Shimoni 1:951, and *Itturey Torah* to Genesis 6:9, among others.

13. Rosenblatt and Horwitz, *Wrestling with Angels*, 66.

14. The parallelism between the creation of Adam and the story of Noah and the Flood is abundantly clear. God began to rebuild the world from a single human being following the destruction, just as the first creation reached its climax with the appearance of Adam. The key difference was that while Adam and Eve were restricted to eating vegetables, Noah and his children were permitted to eat the flesh of animals. God seems resigned to the fact that humankind can be violent and destructive, and therefore postdiluvian human beings need to eat meat to sublimate their basic instincts.

15. In the space of eight verses (Genesis 9:9–17), God mentions the covenant no less than seven times. It sounds like parents going out of their way to reassure their children that they still love them, even though the children may have acted in a less than perfect manner.

16. Steinmetz, "Vineyard, Farm and Garden," 195–196.

17. Noah is the bridge between Adam, who lived ten generations before him and who did not comply with the one command God had given him, and Abraham, who would appear ten generations after Noah. According to the rabbinic tradition, God's covenant with Abraham entailed observing all six hundred and thirteen commandments. See, for example, Pirkei de-Rabbi Eliezer, Chapter 31. The commandments for which Noah was held responsible foreshadowed the full covenant between God and the Jewish people.

18. Genesis 9:20 reads: "And Noah, the farmer, began [*va-yahel*]… and planted a vineyard." Not only does the text emphasize that Noah's first act was the planting of a vineyard, but it also stresses this point of beginning: "Noah began [anew] and planted a vineyard."

19. Devora Steinmetz points out in "Vineyard, Farm and Garden," 200, that God plays no role in the vineyard story. There is a clear increase in the extent of humanity's autonomy and responsibility in each successive story in Genesis. Humans

take on a greater role not only in shaping events but as moral arbiters in the world.

20. B.T. Sanhedrin 70a.

21. According to both rabbinic tradition and modern scholarship, uncovering one's nakedness is a euphemism for some act of sexual immorality. See the comments of Gunther Plaut, *The Torah*, 70, in this regard. Perhaps Ham was guilty of manipulating his father's genitals.

22. The word *arur* ("cursed") appears in the Garden story as well as in the story of Cain and Abel. Similarly, in each of these narratives in Genesis, the plot turns on the importance of fruit: the fruit of the Tree in the Garden, Cain's offering to God of the fruit of the ground, and the vineyard planted by Noah. Ten generations had come and gone between Adam and Noah, but not much had changed in terms of human character. They were still ensconced in their youth.

23. Steinmetz, "Vineyard, Farm and Garden," 205–207.

24. Ibid., 197.

Chapter Four: The People of Shinar (and the Tower of Babel)

1. Shinar is a biblical name for Babylonia. It especially denotes Sumer.

2. Genesis 11:3 reads: "They said to one another." In Hebrew, the phrase implies their closeness and unity of purpose: *'ish 'el rei'eihu*, literally, "a person to his or her friend." Note the use of this phrase elsewhere in Genesis, e.g., Genesis 37:19, where Joseph's brothers are unified by their jealousy of him.

3. The idiom *havah* ("Come, let us…"), which is used with a first person plural verb, appears twice here in two verses: "Come, let us make bricks" (Genesis 11:3) and "Come, let us build us a city" (Genesis 11:4). The emphasis on their unity is accentuated by the superfluous word *lanu* in the phrase "let us build us." The rabbis recognize the sense of unity implied by these phrases when they argue that the Flood generation was destroyed, but the builders of the Tower of Babel were only dispersed because they worked together in peace and harmony. See, for example, Midrash ha-Gadol to Genesis 11:9.

4. Bricks and bitumen were used in Mesopotamia instead of stones and mortar, which were used farther west. Note Gunther Plaut's citation of traditions from Prichard's *Ancient Near Eastern Texts* and from Herodotus' *History* in this

regard. See Plaut's comments in *The Torah: A Modern Commentary*, 80.

5. In this regard, see Peter Pitzele's poignant comments in *Our Fathers' Wells*, 74.

6. Genesis 11:6 reads: "This is how they have begun [*ha-hilam*] to act." The word *ha-hilam* resonates with the Hebrew root *h-l-l*, meaning "to profane." Also, the use of the word *zeh* ("this") is quite pointed and seems to underscore the very disdainful nature of their actions.

7. See Bereshit Rabbah 38:9 for a comparison between the actions of Adam in the Garden and the building of the Tower. The *midrash* plays on the phrase *b'nai Adam* ("human beings" or literally "the children of Adam") in Genesis 11:5.

8. Genesis 11:6 reads: "Nothing they may propose [*yazmu*] to do." The word *yazmu*, from the root *z-m-m*, can mean "to plan, devise, or act in a cunning manner," and the similar word *zimah* means "evil, cunning, or lewdness." Therefore, God's words can be read in different ways.

9. The contrast between the apparent unity of humankind and the real unity in the Godhead can be seen by the parallel use of the phrase *havah* plus a common plural verb in relation to the people of Shinar and God: "Come, let us make bricks" (v. 3), "Come, let us build" (v. 4), and "Come, let us go down and confound" (v. 7).

10. See Midrash ha-Gadol and Rashi to Genesis 11:9 in this regard.

11. Pitzele, *Our Fathers' Wells*, 76–77.

Chapter Five: Abraham

1. Pitzele, *Our Fathers' Wells*, 82.

2. God's words are based on the *midrash* in Bereshit Rabbah 39:7. The rabbis note that, although Terah's death is recorded (in Genesis 11:32) prior to God's call to Abraham, he lived for another 65 years. Terah was 70 years old when Abraham was born, and Abraham departed from Haran at the age of 75, when his father was 145. Terah lived to the age of 205. In the *midrash*, the rabbis portray God as saying to Abraham that the Divine will record the death of his father prior to Abraham's departure from Haran in order to exempt Abraham from the duty of *kibbud av*, which means to honor one's father (seemingly by remaining in his house and caring for him).

3. Pitzele, *Our Fathers' Wells*, 85–87.

4. Ochs, *The Song of the Self*, 68.

5. Ochs, "In the Desert of Our Lives: The Wilderness and Jewish Spirituality" (unpublished manuscript, by permission of the author), 29.

6. Zornberg, *Genesis: The Beginning of Desire*, 74–75. The author notes the tension in Abraham, as underscored in the Ramban's interpretation of Genesis 12:1. On one hand, he feels that he must travel to Canaan in order to complete the family journey. Yet, it is possible that Abraham has no clear idea of his destination. This dialectic is present in all adolescents as they try to clarify their identities and paths in life.

7. Many modern commentators note the power of the phrase *lech lecha* as pointing to Abraham's journey inward, including Samson Raphael Hirsch. See, in this regard, the comments of Aviva Zornberg in *Genesis: The Beginning of Desire*, 74, 87.

8. *Haran* has been taken to mean "route," "journey," or "crossroad." Note, for example, Naomi Rosenblatt's comment in her *Wrestling with Angels*, 96.

9. See Bereshit Rabbah 39:8, in which the rabbis play on the double expression *lech lecha* as if it were to be read *lech lech*, pointing to the two departures of Abraham, one originally from Aram Naharaim and the other from Haran. The rabbis understood that we "leave" more than once in our lives, and that our life journeys develop in stages.

10. The rabbis themselves recognized the difficulty of each aspect, each stage of Abraham's journey from Haran. Note, for example, Bereshit Rabbah 55:7, which compares the stages of difficulty that Abraham experienced in the binding of Isaac (Genesis 22:1: "Take your son, your only son, the one whom you love") to his wrenching departure from Haran.

11. All we are told of the journey of Abraham and his family to Haran is that they set out for the Land of Canaan and arrived there (Genesis 12:5). The reader knows nothing of the arduous nature of this sojourn, which perhaps covered seven hundred miles and must have taken weeks.

12. Genesis 12:9 reads: "Abraham traveled *haloch ve-naso'a* [literally, to and fro], southward."

13. Devora Steinmetz, *From Father to Son: Kinship, Conflict and Continuity* (Louisville: John Knox Press, 1991), 80.

14. The Genesis text states that "[Abram] went down [*va-yaired*] to Egypt. His was a *yeridah*, a spiritual descent, as it was for Judah, when he left his brothers in Genesis 38:1, as indicated in a number of midrashic sources, including Bereshit Rabbah 85:1 and Midrash Ha-Gadol to Genesis 38:1.

15. Abraham's words are based in part on Bereshit Rabbah 40:4.
16. Note the play in Genesis 13:6–7, which states that their possessions were many [*rav*], and as a result a quarrel [*riv*] developed between them. Adolescents often fight over what they own, and Abraham and Lot seem like two siblings engaged in a battle over turf.
17. Sarah's words are based on Bereshit Rabbah 45:6.
18. In Bereshit Rabbah 45:5, R. Judan, in explaining Sarah's remark ("The wrong done to me—*hamasi*—is your fault"), states that Abraham wronged Sarah with words, since he heard her insulted but remained silent. He takes *hamasi* to mean "that which is stolen from me," as if Sarah had complained that Abraham had robbed her of the words that ought to have been spoken on her behalf.
19. The rabbis are even critical of Sarah's immature actions, especially her treatment of Hagar. See, for example, the comments of Radak and Ramban on Genesis 16:6.
20. Steinmetz, *From Father to Son*, 81.
21. Covenant (*brit*) is frequently established through the process of cutting, and smoke and flame often symbolize God's presence. As Gunther Plaut points out in his *The Torah: A Modern Commentary*, 113, this type of covenantal ritual persisted until the time of Jeremiah and probably was a remnant of ancient blood magic, which had assumed legal importance by the time of Abraham.
22. The fact that a deep sleep fell over Abraham seems like a clear reference to Adam in the Garden of Eden. Like Adam, who was given a life-partner, Eve, who represented a promise of the future for him, so, too, did Abraham experience a promise of his future as he lay sleeping. The Covenant between the Pieces refers not only to the future of Abraham's family but also to his own past. As Devora Steinmetz notes in her book *From Father to Son*, 149, the future destiny is not simply imposed upon Abraham and his descendants but takes shape based on Abraham's real-life experiences. As he matures, his future greatness and that of his people become evident.
23. Rosenblatt and Horwitz, *Wrestling with Angels*, 148.
24. Lot is referred to in Genesis 14:14 as Abraham's brother.
25. Abraham's developing relationship with individuals outside his clan is shown by the fact that Eshkol and Aner, neighbors of Abraham when he dwelt by the terebinths of Mamre, are called "his allies" in this passage (Genesis 14:13).
26. Zornberg, *Genesis: The Beginning of Desire*, 113.

27. Note the juxtaposition of Genesis 20:18, in which every womb in the household of Avimelech is opened, and Genesis 21:1, in which we learn that Sarah gives birth.
28. Zornberg, *Genesis: The Beginning of Desire*, 116–117.
29. While Sarah refers to Ishmael as "the son of the slavewoman" (Genesis 21:10), Abraham, by contrast, emphasizes that Ishmael was his son (Genesis 21:11).
30. The text in Genesis 21 literally states that "he [Abraham] cast her [Hagar] off" (Genesis 21:14). It does not say that he sent both of them—Ishmael as well as Hagar—away!
31. Marc Gellman, "After These Things," *Masoret* (Fall 1991): 10.
32. Zvi Adar, *The Biblical Narrative* (Jerusalem: World Zionist Organization, 1959), 123.
33. This is most evident in the description in Genesis 21:3–5 of "Isaac, his son" no less than three times.
34. In this regard, see Peter Pitzele's poignant psychological insights in *Our Fathers' Wells*, 126.
35. The rabbis describe the *Akedah* as the last in a series of ten tests that Abraham had to pass in his lifetime. See, for example, Pirkei d'Rabbi Eliezer, Chapters 26–31.
36. The phrase in Genesis 22:1, "It came to pass after these things," clearly is formulaic, to be translated, "some time afterward." However, the rabbis believed that the juxtaposition of events implied a causal relationship. We could therefore ask: What event(s) preceded the *Akedah* that gave rise to it? What is the relationship between the banishment of Hagar and Ishmael and this final test of Abraham?
37. The *midrash* in Bereshit Rabbah is based on a play on the word *ahar* ("after") in Genesis 22:1. The rabbis read it as similar to the word *harhar*, which means to "think," "reflect," or "muse." They understand Abraham as having misgivings at that moment about the depth of his faith.
38. In Genesis 22:2, the specific sight of the impending sacrifice is not clear. Only upon reaching the land of Moriah could Abraham see the place—God's place—clearly.
39. Though the biblical text tells us nothing of the journey, the rabbis fill in the gaps, describing the obstacles that Abraham faced. See, for example, the many traditions about Abraham's confrontation with Satan on the road to the mountain, particularly Sefer ha-Yashar *Vayera* 44b–45a.
40. Pesiqta Rabbati 40:6.
41. Steinmetz, *From Father to Son*, 82.

42. Rashi comments on Leviticus 1:1 that there is no true revelation if it is not preceded by a "calling"—the use of the verb *karah* (*kuph, reish, heh*). The irony is that although God frequently speaks (*amar*) to Abraham, the only time God ever "calls" to Abraham, when the word *vayikra* is used, comes at the moment when the angel cries out to prevent him from taking Isaac's life. This is the true revelatory moment for Abraham—when he is able to sacrifice his own ego and truly consider the other.

43. Steinmetz, *From Father to Son*, 64.

44. The sequence of events at the beginning of Chapter 23 is not absolutely clear. We do not know whether Sarah died before or after Abraham returned from Mount Moriah, although the implication of the flow of the narrative is that she died after his return. However, since the rabbis emphasize that Sarah died as result of the *Akedah*, it is conceivable that she died upon hearing the news of the intended sacrifice, and this transpired sometime before. We may also argue that the trauma of the impending sacrifice of her only son drove her from her husband's tent in Be'er Sheva, thus accounting for her presence in Kiryat Arba upon Abraham's return. The reader surely would ask why Sarah is situated in Kiryat Arba (and not waiting for her husband and son!) in Be'er Sheva.

45. The text in Genesis 23:2 seems redundant—Abraham is said to have come to Kiryat Arba "to mourn for Sarah and to cry for her." The writer emphasizes here that the patriarch not only went through the formal act of mourning for his wife, but emoted in a very deep way. His emotion is underscored by the fact that the word *livkotah*, "to cry for her," is written with a small *kaf*, thus denoting the uniqueness of his actions.

46. Hagar flees to Be'er Lahai Roi in Genesis 16:14 when she is mistreated by Sarah and, according to the tradition, may have returned there following her banishment in Genesis 21. Interestingly, Isaac is pictured as being in the same place in Genesis 24:62, when Eliezer brings Rebekkah back to be his bride.

47. The rabbis' belief that he married Hagar again is based on their close reading of the text "And Abraham took another wife," which in Hebrew reads *Va-yosef Avraham va-yikah.* The term *va-yosef* is understood as Abraham marrying *again*, namely, to Hagar.

Chapter Six: Isaac

1. The thrust of the rabbinic tradition is that Isaac was 37 years old at the time of the *Akedah*, though some traditions specify other ages. See, for example, the classic passage in Bereshit Rabbah 55:4, as well as the tradition preserved in Pesiqta Rabbati 40:6.
2. The words of Isaac are a re-creation of a portion of an anonymous prose piece in Hebrew written by an Israeli over thirty years ago. It was translated into English by Rabbi Wolli Kaelter.
3. See Bereshit Rabbah 65:10 in this regard, in which the rabbis play on the verse from Genesis 27:1, "Isaac's eyes were too dim to see [*me'ra'ot*]," reading it instead, "Isaac's eyes were dim *from* seeing." What he experienced during the *Akedah*, he carried with him the rest of his life. In fact, the *midrash* adds that when Abraham was about to kill Isaac, tears dripped from the eyes of the angels into Isaac's eyes, thus affecting his eyesight. As a result, his eyes failed him at a relatively young age.
4. Isaac does not descend from the mountain with his father in the biblical narrative. In Genesis 22:19, Abraham is conspicuously alone when he comes down and returns to Be'er Sheva with only his two servants. The fact that the two servants returned *together* (*yachdav*) with Abraham to Be'er Sheva when it was Isaac who walked *together* with his father on the journey to the mountain underscores Isaac's absence.
5. See the insightful comment of Gunther Plaut in *The Torah: A Modern Commentary*, 152.
6. Isaac is conspicuously absent from the story of Sarah's interment in the Cave of Machpelah in Genesis 23. Why did he not return to be there when Abraham buried her in the field of Ephron, the Hittite in Kiryat Arba?
7. In Genesis 25:11–12, the emphasis on Isaac's dwelling in Be'er Lahai Roi is followed by a mention of Ishmael: "And Isaac settled in Be'er Lahai Roi. This is the line of Ishmael." The contiguity of these two phrases perhaps underscores Isaac's connection with Ishmael and Hagar.
8. The rabbis identify Abraham's wife Keturah, mentioned in Genesis 25:1, with Hagar, and further indicate that it was Isaac who went to Be'er Lahai Roi to solidify that relationship. See, in this regard, Bereshit Rabbah 60:14 and 61:4; Midrash Tanhuma Buber; *Chayei Sarah* 9; Pirkei d'Rabbi Eliezer, Chapter 30; and Bereshit Rabbati to Genesis 25:11.

9. During the entire first encounter, Isaac is not pictured by the biblical writer as saying anything, in contrast to Rebekkah.

10. Isaac is truly the first person to "fall in love" in the Bible, and he is certainly the first character to be described as loving another.

11. See the comments of Aviva Zornberg in *Genesis: The Beginning of Desire*, 138–139.

12. The biblical text itself emphasizes that Rebekkah filled the void left in Isaac's life after his mother died by stating that "Isaac brought [Rebekkah] into the tent of Sarah, his mother." Since Sarah never dwelt with Isaac in the region of the Negev close to Be'er Lahai Roi, it is safe to assume that Sarah's tent is used as a metaphor by the biblical writer to mean that Rebekkah had taken Sarah's place in Isaac's life.

13. In this *midrash*, the rabbis also emphasize that the love and compassion was mutual. Rebekkah also prayed to God at that very moment. This tradition is based on a play on the text "Isaac pleaded with the Lord on behalf [*l'nokhah*] of his wife." The term *nokhah*, which actually means "opposite" or "against," is taken to refer to the fact that they were standing (and praying) "opposite" each other.

14. Rosenblatt and Horwitz, *Wrestling with Angels*, 246.

15. Ochs, *The Song of the Self*, 12.

16. In the context of life in Canaan at the time, the stoppage of wells represented an egregious invasion of property rights. As it still is today, water was the most precious commodity in the deserts of the Middle East.

17. Rosenblatt and Horwitz, *Wrestling with Angels*, 232.

18. Isaac's identification with his father is underscored by the biblical text itself. Genesis 25:19 reads: "These are the generations of Isaac, the son of Abraham. Abraham begot Isaac." The text is obviously redundant, emphasizing the relationship between Abraham and Isaac. Isaac was, indeed, his father's son. He was just like him, repeating in fact many of the experiences of his father.

19. Pitzele, *My Fathers' Wells*, 149–152.

20. Rosenblatt and Horwitz, *Wrestling with Angels*, 250–251.

21. After losing his blessing, Esau marries Mahalat, Ishmael's daughter. The rabbis even describe the close relationship between uncle and nephew. See Sefer ha-Yashar 67:8 and Midrash ha-Gadol to Genesis 28:9.

22. The irony is that the father of one of Esau's wives is named Be'eri, meaning "my well." She was a source not of redemption

but of Isaac and Rebekkah's concern about the survival of their family and its unique covenantal relationship with the Divine.

23. Isaac trembled violently as he faced Esau and could barely get out a word. His anxiety is most evident in the words *mi eifo hu*, which challenge any translator. I have rendered them colloquially as "I...Then who?"

24. Rosenblatt and Horwitz, *Wrestling with Angels*, 281.

25. Steinmetz, *From Father to Son*, 99.

Chapter Seven: The Young Jacob

1. Isaac dies and is buried in Hebron at the end of Genesis 35, years after Jacob's return from Laban's house with his large family. More than twenty years have passed since Jacob guilefully stole the blessing that is described in Genesis 27.

2. Ochs, "In the Desert of our Lives," 160.

3. Adin Steinsaltz, *Biblical Images: Men and Women of the Bible* (New York: Basic Books, 1984), 37–38.

4. Steinmetz, *From Father to Son*, 41.

5. Note the play in Genesis 29:10 and 11. Jacob watered [*va-yashk*] the flock and kissed [*va-yishak*] Rachel. In effect, he was willing to respond to her in every way possible. In the process, he sustained her just as he sustained the sheep.

6. Zornberg, *Genesis: The Beginning of Desire*, 207.

7. For an excellent description of Jacob's relationship with Leah, see Zornberg, *Genesis: The Beginning of Desire*, 212.

8. Leah also names Zebulun with the words, "This time, my husband will dwell with me forever, for I have borne him six sons" (Genesis 30:20). The word play is on the root *zbl*, which means "to dwell" or "to live."

9. The Book of Jubilees 36:23.

10. When Jacob says, "Why have you deceived me [*rimitani*]?" he uses the very same word Isaac used to describe his stealing of Esau's blessing in Genesis 27:35: "Your brother came with guile [*mirmah*] and took your blessing." As J. P. Fokkelman noted in *Narrative Art in Genesis* (Amsterdam: Van Gorcum, 1975), 129, the master-deceiver has met his master. Like a boomerang, the word *mirmah* has come back to haunt him.

11. Later, Jacob would describe himself as having left Canaan with nothing more than his staff, but he returns clustered in two camps (Genesis 32:11).

12. Zornberg, *Genesis: The Beginning of Desire*, 205.

13. Ibid., 239.

14. Fokkelman, *Narrative Art in Genesis*, 203–204.

15. Jacob calls himself unworthy, *katonti*, which literally translates as "I am small, the little one." For the first time Jacob admits that he is the younger son, though he carries the blessing of the firstborn.

16. Edward Edinger, *Ego and Archetype* (New York: Penguin Books, 1972), 39.

17. In Genesis 32:31, Jacob named the place of his confrontation with the faceless stranger Penuel, which means "I have seen a divine being face-to-face." He had indeed confronted the Divine as well as the human.

18. This irony is underscored by the fact that when he is asked by the man about his name, he responds, "Jacob." The last time he was asked who he was occurred when he stole the blessing intended for his brother. Then he told his father, Isaac, that he was Esau. Jacob has finally come to grips with who he is and, in the process, is ready to assume his identity as the patriarch of his people.

19. Note how on previous occasions, Jacob always assumed a defensive posture by taking up the rear. See, in this regard, Genesis 32:17.

20. Jacob has abandoned his defensive posture. All he wants now is to gain the favor of his brother. The shift is made clear by the obvious word play in the text. Jacob's entourage is no longer made up of an armed camp, a *mahaneh*; instead, he seeks to find favor, *hen*, in Esau's eyes. The shift is further emphasized by Jacob's offer of a *minhah*, a gift, to Esau.

21. Jacob literally says, "Please accept my blessing [*birkhati*]." It is as if Jacob's gift to Esau is the blessing he once stole from him. See, in this regard, Midrash Sekhel Tov to Genesis 33:11.

22. Plaut, *The Torah: A Modern Commentary*, 222.

23. Rosenblatt and Horwirtz, *Wrestling with Angels*, 302.

24. It is not clear from Genesis 35:27–29 whether Jacob came to Kiryat Arba to visit Isaac and his father subsequently died there, or whether Jacob came there to bury his father. The ambiguity of the biblical account allows for different interpretations.

25. Plaut, *The Torah: A Modern Commentary*, 30–31.

26. Perhaps this hoped-for unity is underscored by the biblical writer in the verses following Reuven's sleeping with Bilhah, which enumerate the twelve sons of Jacob. By listing Reuven first and indicating that he was Jacob's firstborn, which seems superfluous in the list, the text is telling the reader that Reuven still was part of the family and that its unity was not disturbed. In this regard, see Steinmetz, *From Father to Son*, 213.

27. Joseph's primary position in Jacob's eyes is emphasized by the words of Genesis 37:2: "This is the line of Jacob: At seventeen years of age, Joseph tended the flocks." Just when we expect the text to review in chronological order Jacob's progeny, beginning with Reuven and continuing with Leah's sons, we read instead about Joseph and his father's love for him.

28. Thomas Mann, *Joseph and his Brothers*, 320ff.

29. Ibid., 354.

Chapter Eight: The Older Jacob

1. In Genesis 48:7, when Jacob describes Rachel's death prior to his blessing Ephraim and Manasseh, he says, "As for me…she [Rachel] died on me." He explains Rachel's death as a diminishing of his own vital power. See, for example, Seforno's commentary on this verse.

2. Wiesel, *Messengers of God*, 162.

3. The Hebrew name for Egypt, *Mitzraim*, is close to the word *meitzarim*, which means "narrow places" or "places of constraint."

4. In Genesis 42:1–2, Jacob commands his sons to go down to Egypt because there is grain, *shever*, there. The word is repeated three times in these biblical verses, emphasizing its obvious importance in the story. Yet, *shever* has other possible meanings, including "rupture" or "break" as well as "hope." The ambiguity of the words spoken by Jacob, "There is *shever* in Egypt," then point to the irony that Jacob, even unconsciously, has indicated that for all the pain and suffering their journey to Egypt would bring, there is ultimately hope for the family there.

5. The rabbis emphasized that love can upset the natural order of things, as can hate. They pointed to Joseph's act of preparing his own chariot when he had numerous slaves as a primary example of this. Joseph couldn't wait to see his father, whom he loved and missed. See Bereshit Rabbah 55:8 in this regard.

6. Pharoah asks, "How many [*kamah*] are your years?" and Jacob responds as if Pharoah were asking a question about their quality.

7. The text in Genesis 47:9 literally reads, "My years have not reached [*hisigu*] the life-spans of my fathers." *Lehasig* also has a resonance of "attain," thereby hinting at the quality of Jacob's life.

8. The description of Jacob's death in Genesis 49:33 contrasts with the passages that describe Abraham's death (Genesis 25:8)

and Isaac's death (Genesis 35:29). In both of these cases, the words *zaken ve-saveah*, "old and satisfied," are used.

9. Aviva Zornberg points out that this is the first time in the Torah that the word *holeh* ("sick") is used together with the word *hinei* "behold," underscoring the freshness of the perception. See her comment in *Genesis: The Beginning of Desire*, 353.

10. By placing Ephraim and Manasseh upon his knees, blessing them, and promising them a portion of the inheritance, he made them equal to his own sons. See Genesis 48:5–12 in this regard.

11. Several modern interpreters note how ironic it is that at the moment Jacob is about to bless Joseph's sons, he recalls their grandmother, Rachel. Note, in this regard, Steinmetz, *Fathers and Sons*, 129, and Zornberg, *Genesis: The Beginning of Desire*, 375.

12. The verb for crossing his hands is *sikkel*, which can mean both to "act wisely" and "act foolishly." See, for example, Bereshit Rabbah 97.

13. Though Ephraim is placed here before Manasseh, in other biblical passages the order is reversed, indicating their equality. See, in this regard, Numbers 26:28ff and 34:23ff.

14. Rosenblatt and Horwitz, *Wrestling with Angels*, 380.

15. Ibid., 376.

16. Samuel, *Certain People of the Book*, 301.

17. The repetition of the words "gather" and especially "listen" (the word in Hebrew, *shim'u*, is repeated twice) underscores Jacob's purpose in speaking to his sons. He wants them to internalize the fact that they are Israel, a people united in their covenant with the Divine.

18. On the basis of the wording in Genesis 49:2, the rabbis argue that Israel accepted the obligation to recite the *Shema* daily, thus affirming their belief in the God of Israel. See Bereshit Rabbah 98:3–4 in this regard.

19. Levi Meier, *Jacob* (Lanham, Md.: University Press of America, 1994), 55.

20. Ibid., 10–11.

21. Plaut, *The Torah*, 305.

22. Steinmetz, *From Father to Son*, 142.

23. Zornberg, *Genesis: The Beginning of Desire*, 357–358.

24. Perhaps the tension between Jacob and Israel is underscored by Jacob's referring to his sons as "the sons of Jacob" while asking them to "hearken to Israel, [their] father" at the outset

of the blessings in Genesis 49:2. The rabbis stressed that Jacob has not really died. Each of us is Jacob: We continue his life-long struggle for oneness and unity in our lives. See B.T. *Ta'anit* 6b in this regard.

25. As mentioned in Chapter 3, note 17, the tradition usually counts ten generations between Adam and Noah, and another ten between Noah and Abraham.

Postscript: The Life of Joseph

1. Jacob blesses the two boys by saying that through them both his name and the names of his father and grand-father will be recalled. He sees them as a fulfillment of the past and guarantors of the future. See Genesis 48:16.
2. In Genesis 48:15, the text begins the blessing of Ephraim and Manasseh with the words, "And he blessed Joseph, saying...." The blessing of his sons was indeed Joseph's own blessing. See Plaut's comment in this regard in his *The Torah: A Modern Commentary*, 306.
3. Ochs, *Song of the Self*, 69.
4. Steinmetz, *From Father to Son*, 138. The author notes, for example, the parallel between the language used regarding Joseph's conception—"God remembered Rachel and heard her" (Genesis 30:22)—and God remembering Israel in Egypt and hearing their cries of affliction (Exodus 2:24).
5. Both the pit and the prison are called a *bor*. (See Genesis 37:20, 22 and 40:15.) *Bor* means "well," implying also that the pit into which Joseph was thrown, and Egypt itself, were sources of salvation for him. For example, Elie Wiesel, in his *Messengers of God*, 171, alludes to a tradition which describes Joseph as stopping at the pit on his way back from burying his father in the Cave of Machpelah and uttering a blessing. He did this not to remind his brothers of their treatment of him, but rather to express his gratitude to God.
6. Steinmetz, *From Father to Son*, 152.
7. The final word in the Book of Genesis is *b'mitzraim*, "in Egypt." The family is, indeed, in exile, and the end of Genesis is an anticipation of the suffering yet to come. However, the story does not end with words of despair, but rather of hope. The promise to carry Joseph's bones back to the land of Israel hints at the future redemption of the Jewish people.
8. Ochs, *Song of the Self*, 41.

Alter, Robert. *The Art of Biblical Narrative*. New York: Basic Books, 1981.

Cohen, Norman. *Self, Struggle & Change: Family Conflict Stories in Genesis and Their Healing Insights for Our Lives*. Woodstock, Vt.: Jewish Lights Publishing, 1996.

Crain, N.C. *Theories of Development*. Third Edition. New York: Prentice-Hall, 1991.

Crites, Stephen. "The Narrative Quality of Experience," *The American Academy of Religion 39 (1971)*: 291–311.

Diamant, Anita. *The Red Tent*. New York: St. Martin's Press, 1997.

Erikson, Erik H. *Childhood and Society*. Second Edition. New York: W.W. Norton & Co., 1963.

Fokkelman, J.P. *Narrative Art in Genesis*. Amsterdam: Van Gorcum, 1975.

Iser, Wolfgang. *The Art of Reading: A Theory of Aesthetic Response*. Baltimore: Johns Hopkins University Press, 1979.

Josselson, Ruthellen. *Finding Herself: Pathways to Identity Development in Women*. San Francisco: Jossey-Bass, 1987.

Kegan, R. *The Evolving Self: Problem and Process in Human Development*. Cambridge, Mass.: Harvard University Press, 1982.

Kushner, Lawrence. *God Was in This Place & I, i Did Not Know: Finding Self, Spirituality & Ultimate Meaning*. Woodstock, Vt.: Jewish Lights Publishing, 1993.

Lerner, Richard. *Concepts and Theories of Human Development*. Third Edition. New York: McGraw-Hill, 1991.

Mann, Thomas. *Joseph and His Brothers*. Trans. H.T. Lowe-Porter. New York: Alfred A. Knopf, 1944.

Meier, Levi. *Moses—The Prince, the Prophet: His Life, Legend & Message for Our Lives*. Woodstock, Vt.: Jewish Lights Publishing, 1998.

Pitzele, Peter. *Our Fathers' Wells*. San Francisco: HarperSanFrancisco, 1995.

Rosenblatt, Naomi and Joshua Horwitz. *Wrestling with Angels*. New York: Delta, 1966.

Samuel, Maurice. *Certain People of the Book*. New York: Alfred A. Knopf, 1995.

Schuster, Clara Shaw, and Ashburn, Shirley Smith. *The Process of Human Development: A Holistic Approach*. Boston: Little, Brown and Co., 1980.

Steinsalz, Adin. *Biblical Images: Men and Women of the Bible*. New York: Basic Books, 1984.

Visotzky, Burton. *Reading the Book: Making the Bible a Timeless Text*. New York: Schocken, 1996.

Wallerstein, Robert S., and Leo Goldberger, Eds. *Ideas and Identities: The Life and Work of Erik Erikson*. Madison, Ct.: International Universities Press, 1998.

Waskow, Arthur. *Godwrestling—Round 2: Ancient Wisdom, Future Paths*. Woodstock, Vt.: Jewish Lights Publishing, 1996.

Wiesel, Elie. *Messengers of God: Biblical Portraits and Legends*. New York: Random House, 1976.

Zornberg, Aviva. *Genesis: The Beginning of Desire*. Philadelphia: The Jewish Publication Society, 1995.

About Jewish Lights

People of all faiths and backgrounds yearn for books that attract, engage, educate, and spiritually inspire.

Our principal goal is to stimulate thought and help all people learn about who the Jewish People are, where they come from, and what the future can be made to hold. While people of our diverse Jewish heritage are the primary audience, our books speak to people in the Christian world as well and will broaden their understanding of Judaism and the roots of their own faith.

We bring to you authors who are at the forefront of spiritual thought and experience. While each has something different to say, they all say it in a voice that you can hear.

Our books are designed to welcome you and then to engage, stimulate, and inspire. We judge our success not only by whether or not our books are beautiful and commercially successful, but by whether or not they make a difference in your life.

For your information and convenience, at the back of this book we have provided a list of other Jewish Lights books you might find interesting and useful. They cover all the categories of your life:

Bar/Bat Mitzvah	Life Cycle
Bible Study / Midrash	Meditation
Children's Books	Men's Interest
Congregation Resources	Parenting
Current Events / History	Prayer / Ritual / Sacred Practice
Ecology / Environment	Social Justice
Fiction: Mystery, Science Fiction	Spirituality
Grief / Healing	Theology / Philosophy
Holidays / Holy Days	Travel
Inspiration	Twelve Steps
Kabbalah / Mysticism / Enneagram	Women's Interest